SWEET COUNSEL

Mike Bull is a graphic designer who lives and works in the Blue Mountains west of Sydney, Australia. His passion is understanding and teaching the Bible.

SWEET COUNSEL

ESSAYS TO BRIGHTEN THE EYES

MICHAEL BULL

ISBN-13: 978-1502476135
ISBN-10: 1502476134

Designed and typeset by Michael Bull

BIBLE
MATRIX

INTRODUCTION: **BITTERSWEET**   1

CREATION

1 THIS TIME IT'S PERSONAL   11

2 WAR OF THE WORLDVIEWS   19

3 JENGA BIBLE   27

4 RETURN OF THE RAVEN   37

5 THE ETERNAL PEOPLE   45

COVENANT

6 IMAGES OF GOD   59

7 SIMPLY IRRESISTIBLE   71

8 INTERNAL LAW   79

9 CASH AND COVENANT   91

10 I WILL KILL HER CHILDREN WITH DEATH   97

BIBLICAL THEOLOGY

11 BETTER ANGELS   105

12 DOGS AND PIGS   117

13 A TONGUE OF GOLD   127

14 SCALES OF JUSTICE   143

15 SNAKES AND CHAINS   151

SECULARISM

16 ARMED WITH DEATH   159

17 NO COMMON GROUND   169

18 GOD GAVE THEM UP   177

19 LAMECH'S PATSY   195

20 THE EXORCISM OF CHRIST   205

HERMENEUTICS

21 THE PERILS OF DEEP STRUCTURE   213

22 TECHNICIANS AND INTUITIONS   221

23 CURING THE MINDBLIND   233

24 MERCURY RISING   247

25 TOMBOYS AND TOTEMS   259

COVENANT-LITERARY TEMPLATES   269

INTRODUCTION
BITTERSWEET

"Gracious words are like a honeycomb,
sweetness to the soul and health to the body."
(Proverbs 16:24)

If, in the language of biblical symbols, gold is *solid* light and oil is *liquid* light, then honey is liquid gold. As the golden Ark contained the Ten Words, and the oil of the Lampstand lightened the path of the king, so honey is the Word of God in edible form. In the wilderness, manna tasted like honey wafers. In Canaan, the law of the Lord was even more desirable than its precious honey (Psalm 19:10; 119:103).

Bees are used to represent the hosts of the Land, a swarm possessed of a single mind, the Canaanites whose labors would be possessed by Israel. The gift of honey was part of Israel's bittersweet inheritance. Thus bees and honey together perfectly picture the plunder and plagues meted out to Israel under the Law of Moses as blessings and curses, possession or oppression.

You shall inherit their land, and I will give it to you
to possess, a land flowing with milk and honey.
(Leviticus 20:24)

The name of Deborah, "a mother in Israel" who led a successful counterattack against the forces of Jabin king of Canaan and his military commander Sisera, means "bee."[1] For Israel, milk and honey are symbols of the promise of the motherland, the favor of the Father as edible gold for His faithful Son. But not all of Israel's fathers were good.

> Then Jonathan said, "My father has troubled the land. See how my eyes have become bright because I tasted a little of this honey." (1 Samuel 14:29)

It is interesting that honey is found in the mouth of the blessed bride (Song of Solomon 4:11) and on the lips of the cursed harlot (Proverbs 5:3), images of a Covenant kingdom found faithful or unfaithful.

The ministry of bees also illustrates the eternal conversation between the Father and the Son by the Spirit. The Father commands and the Son brings His plans to fruition (John 1:3). The words of the Lord structure all reality, but it is obedience to them which brings life and glory. Just like the Creation of the world, the production of honey is a twofold process of forming and filling. Honeycomb is a many-roomed house. It is filled with glory through the "there-and-back-again" duties of faithful workers who "pollenate" the nations.

Theology should be a similar process. Sadly, so much of it is merely a haphazard collection of separate

---

[1] See also the discussion concerning Samson's honey in "Out Of The Eater," *God's Kitchen: Theology You Can Eat & Drink*, 289.

facts, ideas and opinions, without any consciousness of the wonderful "hive" pattern that is obviously inherent in everything if we have eyes to see.[2]

The fractal "matrix" of the Bible is a framework for understanding the world, and the Covenantal shape of all Scripture is the honeycomb within which all truth is contained. Every theological or natural observation is part of a process of transformation, which finds its origin in the *to-and-fro* of the Trinity. To be truly "filled," theology must first be "formed" by the patterns in the words and works of God.

Douglas Wilson speaks of the "copiousness" of the writer. This is the practice of collecting and recording ideas for later use, much as a bee collects pollen.

> Keep a commonplace book. Write down any notable phrases that occur to you, or that you have come across. If it is one that you have found in another writer, and it is striking, then quote it, as the fellow said, or modify it to make it yours.[3]

> When you collect phrases, points, metaphors, and whatnot in this way, you are, as Cicero used to put it, loaded for bear. By linking "loaded for bear" up with Cicero, incidentally, I am providing another example of the previous point. But this last point is an important part of what the ancient rhetoricians called copiousness.

---

2   See the charts at the end of this book.
3   Douglas Wilson, *Seven Basic & Brief Pointers for Writers*, www.dougwils.com

SWEET COUNSEL

One time G.K. Chesterton, the rolypologist, was patted on the stomach by his adversary, George Bernard Shaw, a beanpole of an infidel, and was asked what they were going to name the baby. Chesterton replied immediately that if it was a boy, John, if a girl, then Mary. But if it turned out to only be gas, they were going to name it George Bernard Shaw. Now we hear that story and marvel at his amazing quickness. And it may well have been such, a prodigy of the moment. But I also wouldn't be a bit surprised to find out that Chesterton had that particular pistol loaded beforehand, and concealed on his person. When copiousness is active, you not only know how to respond in the moment, but you can also see the moment coming, and prepare for it beforehand.

Your commonplace book is just a staging area. You are collecting things in order use them, to get them into your mind and heart, and thence into your writing.[4]

The writer's life is a scavenger's life. This should go also for pastors, teachers, fathers and mothers, and in fact any Christian: all our ministry is didactic and apologetic, discipleship and witness. We collect that we might not only pollenate but also build the kingdom. This means that copiousness alone is not enough. Only kingdom-shaped hearts can hold honey.

This process is exactly what is going on in the wisdom literature and the prophets, and I am constantly amazed at our failure to recognize it. Theirs

---

4 Douglas Wilson, *Uncommon Commonplaces*, www.dougwils.com

was a *biblical* copiousness. Their guns were loaded, their pumps were primed, well before these remarkable minds fired and mouths gushed. All the writers had been Timothys waiting for a Paul to join the dots of the Law with the stylus of the Spirit. Every past event was ammunition for Israel's future. This explains why the book of Revelation is an explosive spray of machine gun fire from a carefully collected and meticulously arranged cache of Old Testament texts.

Biblical copiousness is one thing we love about C. H. Spurgeon. The Bible was his muse. The biblical texts are high walls but they are not lonely, cold, disjointed bricks. Spurgeon preached from the fiery turrets of inspired literature with apparent ease while modern boffins do dog paddle below him in a moat of footnotes and call it scholarship. To these illiterati, the "apostolic hermeneutic" is a marvel and a mystery, an impenetrable keep, when it is simply the result of their biblical copiousness. The cinematic Covenantal ironies of the prophets are lost on the blind guides of today. Jesus and His prophets are far cleverer—and funnier—than even Chesterton. But so many of us do not get their inspired, bittersweet jokes.

Jesus, the Word, created a world where everything "speaks." Every physical object is also mirror and metaphor and lyric and rant; every Covenant-historical event is a self-referencing innovation. Our Lord is the Master of Allusion, and we, as we read the Bible, are to be His commonplace books.

5

If God can quicken and glorify stone by writing on it with His own finger, then how much more will human hearts be glorified, quickened, made alive, and regenerated when the finger of God, the Holy Spirit Himself, writes on them? What is it to be born again? It is to become the Holy Spirit's commonplace book.[5]

The defining feature of the New Israel is legal witness, and as you may be aware, the Greek word for witness is the source of our word "martyr." Honey from the hive is life and death to those who hear it, for it ministers a blessing to the head and a curse to the body. It brightens the eyes but is a sting to the flesh. This was the case with Jonathan, and also with Ezekiel and John.

And he said to me, "Son of man, eat whatever you find here. Eat this scroll, and go, speak to the house of Israel." So I opened my mouth, and he gave me this scroll to eat. And he said to me, "Son of man, feed your belly with this scroll that I give you and fill your stomach with it." Then I ate it, and it was in my mouth as sweet as honey. (Ezekiel 3:1-3)

And I took the little scroll from the hand of the angel and ate it. It was sweet as honey in my mouth, but when I had eaten it my stomach was made bitter. (Revelation 10:10)

Ezekiel and the Revelation are sister books, following the same structure and serving the same purpose: the

5   Douglas Wilson, *Against the Church*, 132.

destruction of Israel, a witness to the nations, and the resurrection of Israel, renewed and made heir to a greater glory. Their message was both bitter and sweet, law and grace, plagues and plunder, death and life. John the Baptist ate locusts and wild honey because his prophecies to a lawless king would bring the consuming armies of Rome and a heavenly country for the "beheaded" saints.

When Christ shared bread and wine with His disciples at Passover, He began their commission as witnesses of things they had heard and seen. The Lord's supper is a bittersweet scroll, honey with a sting, manna for a mustering host. Christ brightens our eyes that we might bear His two-edged sword. We taste and see that He is good, and go out to take possession of His inheritance, the nations.

I hope these short essays not only brighten your eyes but kindle the fire in your belly.

Michael Bull
Katoomba, September 2014

Thanks to Victor Chininin Buele and Chris Wooldridge for proofreading, to Richard Bledsoe, David Robertson and David Deutsch for their encouragement, and kudos to Steven Opp who observed that at the center of a book entitled *Sweet Counsel* there is a tongue of gold.

CREATION

ATHEISTS INSIST ON AN "IMPERSONAL" UNIVERSE DUE TO A LACK OF EVIDENCE FOR A PERSONAL CREATOR, WHILE THEY WILLFULLY REJECT THE PERSONAL TESTIMONY OF THAT CREATOR.

1
THIS TIME
IT'S PERSONAL

One of the most neglected aspects of theology is
the importance to God of legal witness. Not only
is it rarely spoken about in evangelical circles but it is
never mentioned as an answer to the scientistic objections of the day.

For a judgment to be executed, the Law required the
testimony of at least two witnesses (Numbers 35:30;
Deuteronomy 17:6; 19:15). If their stories did not add
up, one or both of them was guilty of "false witness."

> But if he will not hear, take with you one or two
> more, that "by the mouth of two or three witnesses
> every word may be established." (Matthew 18:16)

Based on observations from later "serpent crushings,"
the first two legal witnesses should have been Adam
and Eve: Adam's faithful testimony to the serpent and
Eve's song of triumph after its defeat. Instead, when

given a further opportunity to tell the truth, Adam blamed both God and Eve (unjustly) and Eve blamed the serpent (justly). Instead of faithful witness in the Garden, there was cowardice and cursing.[1]

The next testimony would have been the combined witness of Cain and Abel (as a corporate bride, the first "band of brothers"). They presented the "firstfruits" of the womb and the Land to alleviate the curses pronounced in Genesis 3, that the Lord might pour out the rest of the harvest and vindicate their faithfulness.

Instead of faithful testimony in the Land, innocent blood cried as a silent witness from the ground.

The concept of a double witness, that is, a corroborated testimony, is a common one in the Bible. Not only is the Law itself a double witness (two tablets) but the Law is given twice (two sets of tablets, then Moses giving and re-giving the Law). One wonderful example of a repeated testimony is found in Saul's failure to heed the words of Samuel. When things began to fall apart, and the Lord no longer spoke to Saul, he instead consulted a witch, an "anti-prophet." Ironically, she raised up the spirit of Samuel, who told Saul *exactly what he told him when he was alive,* with an added pronouncement of impending judgment. Since Saul rejected the testimony of the living prophet, his condemnation would be sealed through a second

---

[1] The two tablets in the Ark of the Testimony may represent Adam and Eve, dead in their sins but preserved under a covering of animal blood and awaiting the resurrection of Christ.

Ghost of Samuel appearing to Saul (c. 1800)
William Blake

witness from the dead. The same pattern is found in the condemnation of the Church and State rulers of Jerusalem:

> If they do not listen to Moses and the Prophets, they will not be persuaded even if someone rises from the dead... (Luke 16:31)

At the Transfiguration of Jesus, the Father announced that the testimony of His Son superseded that of the double witness of Moses and Elijah, His previous human representatives. Following this, the resurrection was a sign much like the appearance of Samuel from the dead. Ignorance was no longer an excuse, and the sin would no longer be overlooked. The rejection of the bold legal testimony at Pentecost resulted in the legal witness of the apostles concerning Jerusalem's impending destruction. At every point, the delegation of Covenant authority requires personal legal testimony: the words of God on purified human lips.

In his recent book, *A Shot of Faith [to the Head]*, Mitch Stokes brings to the fore the importance of witness in our understanding of faith. Firstly, he demonstrates that, "Like everyone else, scientists need noninferential basic beliefs. So, lack of evidential support (i.e., the presence of basic beliefs) isn't the difference between faith and science." He then observes that, despite the claims made by atheists that science is based upon "proof" but religion is "believing what you know ain't so," the faith of the saints in the

Bible has an aspect which they overlook: it is a dependence upon a reliable, legal witness. Stokes writes:

> The substance of Abraham's faith was that he simply believed what God told him, despite the apparent improbabilities (Romans 4; Hebrews 11:8-11). Biblical faith is taking God at His word, trusting what He says. Faith is believing God's *testimony*.
>
> And this is the sense of "faith" that John Locke used in the original context of evidentialism. For Locke, faith is "the assent to any proposition, not thus made out by the deductions of reason, but upon the credit of the proposer, as coming from God in some extraordinary way of communicating." Faith, again, is believing something on the say-so of God himself, rather than by way of an argument (i.e., rather than "by the deductions of reason"). Although I might be able to impressively argue that Jesus is the Son of God, if I believed this doctrine only by way of my arguments, I wouldn't be simply taking God at his word. I wouldn't believe by way of faith, but, rather, by way of reason...
>
> We can now define "faith" as follows: Faith is believing something by way of testimony.[2]

Atheists insist on an "impersonal" universe due to a lack of evidence for a personal Creator, while they willfully reject the *personal testimony* of that Creator. Thus, they are requiring from God something that is against His very nature, and indeed, against the nature

2 Mitch Stokes, *A Shot of Faith [to the Head]*, 29-31.

of humans made in His image. We are called to believe the *witness* of Christ and His Spirit, and of the prophets and apostles, precisely because the very nature of reality is personal.

Moreover, a legal testimony concerns not only the works of the one being testified about, but also rests upon the character of the witness. The rejection of the Bible is thus a slur against Christ's character, who not only speaks but *is* the truth, and can swear only by Himself because there is none greater. It is also the character assassination of His holy witnesses, the *martyrs*, whose writings are considered "perjurious."

Atheism's demand for *impersonal* evidence results from the rejection of the testimony of a *specific* Person. With the mouth of God silenced, scientism then objectifies everything in Creation (including humans) that Creation might not "speak" of its Creator. With both the spoken and silent witnesses censored, it then asserts that there is no evidence for an impersonal, objectified god. This is correct, because God is not only personal but also inscrutable aside from His words and deeds. As it was in Eden, the rebellion is *personal*—the unwillingness to honor God's words due to a mistrust of His character.

Modern scientism is the result of the false witness of geologist and lawyer Charles Lyell (1797–1875), who desired to "free science from Moses."

Lyell, the lawyer *par excellence*, was involved, not in scientific investigation but political game playing to ensure his uniformitarian ideas would be accepted by the church, even though he *knew* they clearly contradicted the plain teaching of Scripture. Lyell's secretive scheming not only deceived the church to accept his false ideas that undermined the Gospel, but he set geology on a wrong path for over a century, as geologists now recognize...[3]

The rejection of the testimony of Moses is not only the rejection of true science, but also of the witness of the one who rose from the dead, the testimony of Jesus. Without Moses there is no Gospel.

The repression of the truth (both spoken and silent witnesses) results in further darkness (Romans 1:18). If His words are rejected, God deliberately *hides* Himself from the disobedient, as He hid himself from Saul. Those who will not hear will not see. When they do finally hear and see, it will be because it is too late.

The love or hatred of Christ is always personal. The judgment will likewise be personal, and the legal testimony will be spoken by human lips. The words that seal a man's destiny will be spoken by an enthroned Man, the Law of Moses written on flesh, fulfilled in a Person. He will refer to His own testimony and that of the apostles and prophets, and personally speak an eternal blessing or an eternal curse.

3   David Catchpoole and Tas Walker, *Charles Lyell's hidden agenda—to free science "from Moses,"* www.creation.com

H. G. WELLS
WAS AN
OPTIMIST,
BUT DIED
IN DESPAIR,
BETRAYED BY
DARWINISM.

2
WAR OF THE WORLDVIEWS

"There is a curse on Mankind.
We may as well be resigned
to let the devil, the devil
take the spirit of man."

I was eleven when I first heard Jeff Wayne's musical version of *The War of the Worlds*. It was electric and terrifying. Hearing it again years later, the worldview behind the story is much more apparent. One song in particular lays it bare: *The Spirit of Man*.

The madness of Parson Nathaniel (or in the novel, the Curate) is presented as a symptom of the failure of religion to cope with the "brave new world" of modern men. To the parson, the invading martians are devils incarnate. His worldview is mistaken and he is unable to come to terms with the exposure of its illegitimacy. He has misinterpreted the world.

SWEET COUNSEL

THE DEMONIC REBRANDED

The musical added the character of his wife, Beth, to serve as a counterpoint to his insane resignation. She argues,

> *"But they're not devils, they're martians."*

Interestingly, one of the paintings in the original double LP album booklet mimics "The Temptation of St Anthony" by Salvador Dali. Parson Nathaniel is positioned as St Anthony, holding up his crucifix as a defense against the invaders. The Martians tower above him in their tripod vehicles, which are metal versions of Dali's strange elephants with stilt-like legs.

It is Parson Nathaniel, however, who is correct in this case. There is no place for angels or demons in a brave new world, so the beings from the stars are devils renamed. The testimonies of many who have had close encounters with such "extraterrestrials" are chilling, and clearly of a spiritual nature.[1]

Beth attempts to draw Nathaniel back to reason with a plea to place his hope in the goodness of mankind.

> *"If just one man could stand tall*
> *There would be some hope for us all*
> *Somewhere, somewhere in the spirit of man."*

---

[1] See Gary Bates, *Alien Instrusion: UFOs and the Evolution Connection.*

The Temptation of St. Anthony (1946)
Salvador Dalí

SWEET COUNSEL

So Parson Nathaniel is the doomsayer, the epitome of nineteenth century theology, whence came the various apocalyptic scenarios which still plague us today. He believes in the power of the devil but *denies* the power of the ascended Christ. Beth is the secular humanist, the one who believes true humanity can provide its own Messiah, one who is able to "stand tall" *without* the power of the ascended Christ.

In this "culture war in song," both Nathaniel and Beth are wrong. Both deny Christ. It is the absent postmillennialist who is right. The demons are real, but they are not to be feared. Christ is reigning now and will reign until all His enemies are under His feet.

BITTER FRUIT

The story begins with the Martians "scrutinizing" us like creatures that swarm and multiply in a drop of water. In the end, of course, it is the bacteria of earth against which the Martians have no defense. They are wiped out by something they overlooked, something which seemed too weak and insignificant for concern. This is the Church of Christ. While proud men plan, build, legislate and exploit, and exalt their ideologies against the knowledge of God, the body of Christ is invisibly swarming and multiplying.

The "brave" ideas of the nineteenth century which brought havoc upon the twentieth are now wearing thin. After 150 years of desperate digging, the theory of evolution is quickly running out of excuses. The

Zionist doomsayers and their paralyzing interpretations of the Bible are finally being exposed as false prophets. The atheists offered false hopes and the doomsayers painted bleak pictures, but the microscopic yeast of the Gospel spells doom for them both. The heresies of the nineteenth century will be put to rest.

The Church of Christ has outlasted the "brave new world" and is booming in the global south while the northern countries which embraced these scientistic heresies slowly disintegrate.

"Heresies are experiments in man's unsatisfied
search for truth." – H. G. Wells

H. G. Wells was an optimist, but died in despair, betrayed by Darwinism. Like a Martian, he regarded less developed cultures as "creatures that swarm and multiply in a drop of water." Jerry Bergman writes:

After being exposed to Darwinism in school, H.G. Wells converted from devout Christian to devout Darwinist and spent the rest of his life proselytizing for Darwin and eugenics. Wells advocated a level of eugenics that was even more extreme than Hitler's. The weak should be killed by the strong, having "no pity and less benevolence." The diseased, deformed and insane, together with "those swarms of blacks, and brown, and dirty-white, and yellow people ... will have to go" in order to create a scientific utopia. He envisioned a time when all crime would be punished

23

by death because "People who cannot live happily and freely in the world without spoiling the lives of others are better out of it." He was hailed as an "apostle of optimism" but died an "infinitely frustrated" and broken man, concluding that "mankind was ultimately doomed and that its prospect is not salvation, but extinction. Despite all the hopes in science, the end must be 'darkness still'." Wells' life abundantly illustrates the bankruptcy of consistently applied Darwinism.[2]

Wells misinterpreted the world. His own atheistic ideas were the heresies, and they bore a bitter fruit in his life, just as they have in our culture. In God's providence, this fruit is part of the relentless exposure in history of all the godless ideas born "somewhere in the spirit of Man."

---

2   Jerry Bergman, "H. G. Wells, Darwin's Disciple and Eugenicist Extraordinaire," *Journal of Creation,* 18 (3):116-120, December 2004

GENESIS 1 IS CERTAINLY "TEMPLE-STRUCTURED," BUT IT'S NOT MERELY AN INAUGURATION SERVICE, AND ADAM IS NOT CHOSEN FROM AMONG HIS BROTHERS.

3
JENGA BIBLE

Some theistic evolutionists argue that the Creation narrative does not describe physical acts of Creation but rather acts of "Covenantal delegation."

Interpreting the Creation account as a process of conferring the authority of "Temple purposes" to a physical Creation already in existence allows them to maintain that the narrative contains some measure of historical truth without rejecting the long ages asserted by naturalism.[1] Besides the deep logical problems this causes, the assertion also reveals an ignorance of the nature and shape of biblical Covenants.

THE CALL OF ADAM

Within this framework, Daniel Harrell asserts that Adam and Eve were not the first real people, but the first people *with whom God entered into a Covenant relationship*.

---

1   See John H. Walton, *The Lost World of Genesis One: Ancient Cosmology and the Origins Debate*.

For many Christians, the biblical characters Adam and Eve can present a significant challenge to accepting evolutionary theory—that is, when they are cast as historical figures who are also the biological progenitors of the human race. ...the Rev. Daniel Harrell discusses how there may be some "middle ground" in the way that Christians understand Adam and Eve. Harrell points out that the historicity of Adam and Eve does not necessarily conflict with science. Rather, the claim that conflicts with science is the idea that Adam and Eve were the first humans, who were the only original biological ancestors of all humans today.

Instead, another way to view them is as the first two people with whom God chose to enter into a covenant relationship, like He did with Abraham, for example. In this view, Adam and Eve become representative of the kind of relationship that God intends to have with all people. This may be a point of possible convergence, says Harrell, "for those who are worried about a historical Adam and Eve to breathe easier, and those who are concerned about integrity with DNA and evolutionary science to also breathe easier."[2]

Harrell's interpretation might seem viable to the undiscriminating, but in reality it is a game of "kick the can." The problem isn't resolved. Rather, like the ring around the bath in *The Cat-in-the-Hat Comes Back*, it simply moves the problem elsewhere, leaving traces of its dirty mark throughout the rest of the Bible.

Firstly, the Bible does not describe a "separation" of

---

2   *Daniel Harrell on Adam and Eve,* biologos.org

Adam from other people, but distinct and unique acts for the origin of the man and his wife. To assert that this is symbolic language for a "choosing" of Adam from among his brothers is to ignore what the text actually says. Not only did God create Adam from the dust, but the text which describes this process recapitulates the Creation Covenant of Genesis 1.[3]

Secondly, since this claimed separation of Adam from other humans was a Covenantal act, it puts all other humans living at the time *outside* this Covenant. This assertion contradicts the processes found in later Bible history. Each such "choosing" from among men is based upon previous Covenant faithfulness, resulting in the commissioning of the chosen one and the disinheriting of the unfaithful. For there to have been a Covenantal "disinheriting" of the non-Adamites at the beginning of the Adamic Covenant, the previous race must have been under some sort of Covenant from their physical Creation.

Unless this first era was nothing like any later era, *why* were they disinherited? All of Harrell's non-Adamites died without hope under the Sanctions of a previous Covenant which is either not recorded for us, or which *they were never given.* If, instead, they were "not-quite-human-enough," how could Adam have been chosen from among them without some sort of creative act? We are left with either the question of the nature of the previous "Creation" Covenant and its

3   See the chart at the end of this chapter.

The Temptation and Expulsion of Adam and Eve (1508-1512)
Michelangelo, The Sistine Chapel

Sanctions, or forced to admit some kind of miraculous transformation. The problem is not resolved, just moved or maintained. The assertion displays a profound ignorance, not of the actual text of the Bible, but an ignorance of the shape, the careful integration, and significance of the various parts of that text.

Thirdly, the Sanctions of the Covenant we *are* told about are a choice between fertility and dominion, or physical death. If the world had already known not only suffering and death, but also historical continuity (the fruit of the land and the fruit of the womb), for millions of years, these Covenant Sanctions are entirely redundant. And this is beside the fact that God could call such a corrupted Creation "good," which is a slur upon His omnipotent judgment.

THE SONS OF GOD

Establishing a new genealogy by Covenant has ramifications in subsequent history. One theory is that the non-Adamites were those with whom the "sons of God" intermarried in Genesis 6. However, we don't need to invent non-Adamites to have an intermarriage between Covenant people and people outside the Covenant. The "daughters of men" were descendants of Cain and his followers, children of Adam who had distanced themselves from the Adamic priesthood.

Genesis 6 records the syncretization of two *Adamic* kingdoms (Sethites and Cainites), not an intermarriage of Adamic and non-Adamic races. God wiped out all humanity with the flood because all were descendants of Adam and thus under the Covenant described in Genesis 1-2. The genealogies make this clear.

Once again, this theory ignores the details of the text to accommodate a pagan philosophy of origins.

THE CALL OF ABRAM

A related idea is that the Covenant established in these "Adamites" in Genesis 1-2 was the beginning of the Hebrew people. Certainly, it was the beginning of a history which was continued in the lineage of Abraham, but the assertion that this first Covenant was the separation and beginning of the priestly people as distinct from the pagans shows a fundamental misunderstanding of the Bible.

There were no "Hebrews" until God tore humanity in two by initiating Circumcision after Babel. The bipolarity began not with Adam but with Abraham and ended with the destruction of the Jewish Temple in AD70. If Adam were not the head of the entire race, this later division has little meaning. The Hebrew lineage was not begun in Adam. Its genealogy was begun in Abraham and its priesthood was established under Moses and Aaron.

Moreover, the Abrahamic Covenant was established to be a blessing to the nations which developed after the flood, for whom we have genealogies which trace their origins to Noah, not to "non-Adamites."

TOWER TO HEAVEN

This theorizing is carried out by qualified theologians who show little respect for the actual text of the Bible and whose cherry-picking seems largely ignorant of the internal logic of the Scriptures.

Genesis 1 is certainly "Temple-structured," but it is not merely an inauguration service, and Adam is not chosen from among his brothers. The text says he was created from the dust in a Creation unmarred by sin. There is not a single non-Adamite to be seen. All of us are Adamites.

> Therefore, just as sin came into the world through one man, and death through sin, and so death spread to all men because all sinned... (Romans 5:12)

> For as in Adam all die, so also in Christ shall all be made alive. (1 Corinthians 15:22)

An actual, physical, historical "Construction of Creation by Covenant" is inescapable. Any attempt to shift the foundations of the Bible is to play Jenga with Covenant history, which is a carefully constructed tower to heaven. Basic logic dictates that these wishful interpreters must either reject the Genesis account or settle for Adam being the first actual man.

TRANSCENDENCE

"...then the Lord God
(Day 1 / Ark / Sabbath)

HIERARCHY

formed the man
(Day 2 / Veil / Passover)

ETHICS

of dust from the ground
(Day 3 / Altar & Table / Firstfruits)

and breathed into his nostrils
(Day 4 / Lampstand / Pentecost)

the breath of life,
(Day 5 / Incense / Trumpets)

OATH/SANCTIONS

and the man became
(Day 6 / Mediators / Atonement)

SUCCESSION

a living creature."
(Day 7 / Godlikeness / Booths)

(Genesis 2:7)

THE WORD
OF THE LORD
NEVER RETURNS
TO HIM EMPTY,
EVEN WHEN
THAT WORD IS
A CURSE.

4
RETURN OF
THE RAVEN

BIRD'S EYE VIEW

Events viewed out of context are events without meaning. Interpreting a chapter isolated from a book or a scene isolated from a movie is not a recipe for success. We are forced to read purpose into them based upon our own presuppositions, our own context.

This is part of the reason why moderns have such trouble with the Bible. We have been taught to read it by men who have no sense of narrative. Placing an image outside its usual context renders it an open invitation for the reader to fill the hole with whatever seems right in his own eyes.

Here's an example. Genesis 8, with no explanation of Noah's reasoning, tells us that the prophet sent out a raven. The modern might wonder what was going through Noah's mind? The question of whether or not the raven returned might also be raised. Was the raven sent first because it was unclean and therefore a less valuable animal to preserve for the new world? Or was it sent first because it was a stronger bird? Does the phrase *"to and fro"* suggest a single outward journey and return? Or did the bird not return, eating and resting upon floating corpses, as Luther suggests? All sorts of Jewish and Christian sources might be quoted, but it seems to me that we have isolated the event, and thus missed its significance.

The Church possesses the complete Word of God, and thus has a "bird's eye view" of all Bible history. If we are open to the idea of one story being told over and over again in different ways, using different "raw materials," we are not left to ponder Noah's state of mind.

Since the Spirit of God was at work in Noah's prophetic ministry, it is likely Noah was thinking God's thoughts. But how can we know God's thoughts? We can see the same action taking place in other places in the Bible, and the clue is not so much the "raw materials" (in this case, two birds) as the common structure, the consistent "process" of God's work in the world.

THE DAY OF COVERINGS

The chain of events in the Garden of Eden follows a sevenfold pattern, which then becomes the first cycle in a sevenfold history, taking us from Adam to Noah, from the beginning of the first world to the beginning of a new one.

Noah, Mosaic in Basilica di San Marco, Venice

Moreover, this pattern prefigures the annual feasts of Israel. In Eden, the Day of Atonement was the Spirit of the Lord moving *"to and fro"* searching for Adam and Eve "in the Spirit of the Day." Blood was shed and the Land was rendered clean. Man moved from the Garden into the Land and began to farm.

In the greater pattern (Adam to Noah), the Day of Atonement is the flood. Once again blood was shed and the Land was rendered clean.

This connection between eyes, ravens, obedience to God (Father) and the Church (Mother), and the Lord's subsequent blessing upon the Land turns up in some strange places. Here's one that puts a Noahic spin on one of the Ten Commandments, the one which concerns an Israelite honoring his father and mother that he might live long in the Land:

> The eye that mocks a father
> and scorns to obey a mother
> will be picked out by the ravens of the valley
> and eaten by the vultures.
> (Proverbs 30:17)

The High Priestly rite of atonement, established by the Lord many centuries later, is the same process in miniature. The Urim and Thummim, a white stone and a black stone hidden in the ephod, communicated the mind of the Lord concerning the offering. A white stone indicated that the offering had been accepted and the Land was once again considered clean by the Lord for another year. (The Jerusalem Talmud records that a black stone was drawn every year after the death of Christ until the destruction of the Temple, indicating that the animal sacrifices were no longer accepted by God. The Land was considered unclean and ripe for judgment.[1])

In Hebrew, the word "redeemer" is twofold. It means both avenger and redeemer, like the twin stones in the pouch on the Day of Coverings. This is because the Lord *destroys* His enemies to *rescue* His people. The black and white stones served the same purpose legally as the black and white birds served physically.

So, the black bird represents the eyes and mouth of the destroyer. He is unclean because he has the job of cleaning up the mess, eating death just like the serpent eats (Adamic) dust. The bodies of the cursed were not buried ("covered") but remained exposed to be eaten by birds and beasts. We hear similar words from the mouth of Goliath, curses which filled David with righteous indignation, since Goliath was cursing the children of Abraham (Genesis 12:3).

As the black bird moved *"to and fro"* like the eyes of God, scanning the face of the waters, so the white bird searched for a holy remnant of the old world to save and carry into the new: "The Branch."

---

[1]   "Forty years before the destruction of the Temple, the western light went out, the crimson thread remained crimson, and the lot for the Lord always came up in the left hand. They would close the gates of the Temple by night and get up in the morning and find them wide open." Jacob Neusner, *The Yerushalmi*, 156-157.

A WHEEL FULL OF EYES

Not only can we read this dual act of blessing and cursing back into the history of Noah, we can read it forward into the book of Revelation, which takes just about every Covenant/festal cycle in the Bible and rolls them all together into an amazing tapestry of Israel's history, one giant Covenant cycle, a wheel full of eyes.

Revelation 19 is the end of the story of two women, or rather, two sides of the same woman. The Gospel of Jesus goes out as four horsemen and divides the Jews into two camps: those who received the Spirit (the Dove, like David) and those who rejected Him, and received an evil spirit instead (like Saul). The choice for the Jews was not, in their mind, a choice concerning God, but a choice concerning who was His representative. It was a choice between two kings, between Herod and Jesus, Christ and antichrist. This choice of who was their head was the beginning of a Covenant cycle like that which began with Adam and ended with Noah. At the end of the process, the body was divided. Or rather, there were two bodies. The holy remnant was a chaste bride and the rest of Israel was an exposed harlot. Revelation 19 speaks of the harlot being eaten by scavenging birds while the true bride dined with her Bridegroom in heaven. The members of the true bride were gathered and purified by the Dove, the Holy Spirit, and she was invited to eat with God. The harlot was dismembered, scattered into pieces, and eaten by the unclean servants of God.[2] It was much like the days of Noah.

Of course, the raven did return to his mate eventually. We still have ravens. And the Word of the Lord never returns to Him empty, even when that Word is a curse.

---

2   These were the same servants of God who, ironically and miraculously, fed (blessed) Elijah in the wilderness while God's rebellious people were cursed with a famine.

ALL GOD'S
DARLINGS END UP
ON THE ALTAR.
THERE IS NO
ETERNAL PEOPLE.

5
THE ETERNAL PEOPLE

THE DREAMTIME IS OVER

The Bible teaches us that flesh is temporary. This is bad news for those who distrust God. Flesh is all they have.

Throughout the millennia, families and tribes have recited the genealogies of their past, and struggled to produce enough children to secure a cultural future. The bloodline of unseen ancestors and bright-eyed offspring, past and future, was reinforced, thread by thread, in stories around the fires of "now." This wasn't the romantic picture so often painted for us. The struggle for cultural survival also involved blood and fire outside the camp.

David P. Goldman observes that in the ancient world a continual state of conflict would account for a loss of two per cent of the population every year, and that this would also explain the proliferation of languages and dialects. He writes that even in Christianity's darkest hours (which were simply tribalism on a grander scale), it failed to kill a small fraction of the proportion which routinely and normally fell in primitive warfare. He quotes Nicholas Wade's *Before the Dawn,* "a survey of genetic, linguistic, and archeological research on early man":

> Even in the harshest possible environments, where it was a struggle enough just to keep alive, primitive societies still pursued the more overriding goal of killing one another... casualty rates were enormous, not the least because they did not take prisoners. That policy was compatible with their usual strategic goal: to exterminate the opponent's society.[1]

Of course, we see a similar emphasis on succession in the Old Testament. The fulfillment of the promises to Abraham was directly related to Israel's continuity.

Goldman's point is that the "primitive authenticity" taught in modern Western institutions is a fraud. In an attempt to avoid further damage to the environment, our children are being indoctrinated with the idea that aboriginal cultures worldwide, left to themselves, would have been self-sustaining, perhaps indefinitely, in an eternal cycle of life and death:

---

[1] David P. Goldman, "The Fraud of Primitive Authenticity" in *It's Not the End of the World, It's Just the End of You: The Great Extinction of the Nations,* 90-91.

You have noticed that everything an Indian does is a circle, and that is because the Power of the World always works in circles, and everything and everything tries to be round.

In the old days all our power came to us from the sacred hoop of the nation and so long as the hoop was unbroken the people flourished. The flowering tree was the living center of the hoop, and the circle of the four quarters nourished it. The east gave peace and light, the south gave warmth, the west gave rain and the north with its cold and mighty wind gave strength and endurance. This knowledge came to us from the outer world with our religion.

Everything the power of the world does is done in a circle. The sky is round and I have heard that the earth is round like a ball and so are all the stars. The wind, in its greatest power, whirls. Birds make their nests in circles, for theirs is the same religion as ours. The sun comes forth and goes down again in a circle. The moon does the same and both are round. Even the seasons form a great circle in their changing and always come back again to where they were.

The life of a man is a circle from childhood to childhood, and so it is in everything where power moves. Our teepees were round like the nests of birds, and these were always set in a circle, the nation's hoop, a nest of many nests, where the Great Spirit meant for us to hatch our children.

Black Elk, Holy Man of the Oglala Sioux, 1863-1950

Without exception, European migration around the world devastated tribal peoples. Colonists committed many atrocities, but our children are taught that the cultures in the conquered lands were somehow pristine, natural, balanced, sustainable—*eternal.*

With a worldview informed by biblical history, and indeed secular history, these "eternal cycles" are exposed as a downward spiral. The gradual degradation of ancient cultures and the loss of even primitive skills within these cultures has been well-documented. Paganism moves in circles, but if the fact of sin and the necessity of redemption are rejected, there is no eternity, not even a carnal "cultural" one. A civilization is a corporate Man. All men die. All civilizations die.

No culture is all good or all bad. For instance, despite its spiritual darkness, there is much traditional wisdom in native American culture. Huguenot adventurer Jean de Lery had great admiration for the natives, who seemed to be more virtuous than Europeans. In many ways the "primitive" worldviews of native Americans in the both north and south are more biblical than that of modern Christians, containing many elements which can be easily traced to their origin in the book of Genesis. However, spiritual history has moved on, and these cultures are merely ancient minds "preserved in amber." The continuing work of God often leaves our "timeless truths" in the dust.

History moves in cycles, but there is always either regress or progress. Culture moves forwards or it moves backwards. All the indigenous cultures of the world, at the point they had reached when white men arrived, were "backward," but backwardness is not a solid state. Life was a constant battle to avoid extinction. We can learn from the wisdom of any culture, including the tribal ones, but left to themselves, indigenous cultures would have continued to degenerate to the point of oblivion.

The idea of growth, progress and dominion is a Christian one. The Biblical history moves from family, to tribe, to people, to nation, to kingdom, to empire. When the enormous granite wheels of empire came into contact with the slowing spinning tops of tribal life, there could be no "cog wheel" correspondence. The results were tragic.

Before our white brothers arrived to make us civilized men, we didn't have any kind of prison. Because of this, we had no delinquents. Without a prison, there can be no delinquents.

We had no locks nor keys and therefore among us there were no thieves. When someone was so poor that he couldn't afford a horse, a tent or a blanket, he would, in that case, receive it all as a gift.

We were too uncivilized to give great importance to private property. We didn't know any kind of money and consequently, the value of a human being was not determined by his wealth.

We had no written laws laid down, no lawyers, no politicians, therefore we were not able to cheat and swindle one another. We were really in bad shape before the white men arrived and I don't know how to explain how we were able to manage without these fundamental things that (so they tell us) are so necessary for a civilized society.

John (Fire) Lame Deer, Sioux Lakota, 1903-1976

When colonists arrived, with their greed and diseases, things changed forever. These were deep cuts, but perhaps the most fatal was the change in philosophy. Cycles were out, and progress was in, a mindset which was born, arguably, of the "marriage-made-in-heaven" of Roman imperialism and the Great Commission. "Modernity" had arrived, and there was no way back. Despite the desperate efforts of tribal elders worldwide, attempts to revive and maintain the ancient animisms and languages have resulted in little more than nostalgic historical records, ornamental subcultural identities, and tourist exhibits.[2] The old spirits are gone.

After a backlash by indigenous Australian cultures in the 1970s against the Christian missions, and a return to animism, the more objective Aboriginal leaders are facing the fact that this was a backward step for their people. Whatever the crimes of the colonists, and whatever the excesses of the missions, the leaven of Christianity which they brought with them forces any culture, any people, to rise, to grow up. It calls us from

2   Goldman also argues that Islamic fundamentalism is not offensive but defensive, a futile attempt by religious leaders to stem the inevitable secularization of modern Muslim nations.

Murzu nomadic cattle herder, Ethiopia.   Image: urosr / Shutterstock.com

animistic childhood to adulthood, from a world ruled by animals to a world subdued by men. Our eyes are opened in a greater way to both good and evil and a judicial maturity is forced upon us. In many cases, indigenous people were not ready, but a return to the "childish things" of animism is impossible. The Gospel destroys tribal divisions and animistic thinking. Once the Gospel wakes you up, the Dreamtime is over.

John Lame Deer certainly has a case against civilization, but he is judging civilization through eyes *opened* by civilization. Worse, he is looking through the rose-colored glasses of nostalgia. John Wesley made a survey of human societies to see if any had overcome the effects of sin. Thomas C. Oden writes:

> Among native American cultures with whom he had some immediate experience, [Wesley] observed as evidence of sin their constant intertribal warfare. He was especially disturbed by their practice of torturing defenseless victims. As one of the few English writers of his day who had actually spent time in the immediate environment of native American Indians, Wesley did not share the distantly conceived inflated picture of the noble savage that prevailed among enlightened French *literati* of the 18th century. Wesley punctured this picture mercilessly, providing a graphic depiction of how these natives were as deeply embedded in sin as the avaricious colonial British.[3]

---

3   Thomas C. Oden, *John Wesley's Scriptural Christianity*, 163.

The preciousness of tribal life, in truth, rendered all life cheap. Tribes were cultures bent on self-preservation through bloody rivalries. A similar insanity might be observed in modern cultures, where the deaths of endangered species make the news but the culling of human lives through various means is considered a matter of survival. Goldman believes the fraud of primitive authenticity, the modern nature worship of environmental "animism," is the environmentalist projecting his own presentiment of death onto the natural world.

> Fear for the irreversible destruction of the natural world ... substitutes for the death anxiety of the individual. Post-Christian Westerners confound their own sense of mortality with the vulnerability of the natural world. Sadly, it is not the end of the world. It is just the end of you.[4]

There is a perverse logic to this projection. In God's wisdom, the flesh of the world *and* the flesh of Man are bound together by Covenant. Environmentalists believe their own flesh is a cancer upon the flesh of the otherwise "eternal" world, but the Bible tells us that Man and World are bound together for a purpose. The voyage of discovery is also a process of *self*-discovery. Subduing the world, however destructive it might be, is a *positive* feature of Man. Man and World are bound together not only for death, but also for resurrection.

4   Goldman, 183.

By showing us that true eternity transcends cultural longevity, the Gospel of Christ removes the fear of death (Hebrews 2:15). This means that, since the resurrection, the fear of mortality for both the individual and the culture (and indeed, the planet) is now a "drawing back" from God's desire for us. This is a lesson which Christendom failed to learn, and the factor which subsequently tore it apart.

Goldman observes that many minor cultures facing extinction found cultural transcendence in Christianity. However, their failure to leave pagan superstitions entirely behind perpetuated the old fractures, and led to a desire for *nationalistic* transcendence in a Christian veneer. Every European culture considered itself to be "the eternal people" to some degree. The American experiment succeeded because the old paganisms and nationalisms were deliberately left behind.

> For all its flaws and fecklessness, America remains in the eyes of its people an attempt to order a nation according to divine law rather than human custom, such that all who wish to live under divine law may abandon their ethnicity and make themselves Americans.[5]

America is unique. It is not a redeemed culture but a melting pot of cultures. For Americans to backslide, they had to *invent* somewhere to slide, hence the liberal agenda and its historical revisionism (including

5   Goldman, 372.

naturalism). It is a manufactured pagan past disguised as a future.

America is not eternal. To keep His promises, God cannot allow it to be. For the sake of greater glory, the American vision is fading. However, the unmistakable success of the American experiment reveals it to be a microcosm for the future of the world—all nations submitting willingly to the Divine Law.

Goldman sees the continued historical perseverance of the Jewish identity as evidence of God's promise to the rest of mankind, and here is where we part ways.

There cannot be an eternal people, not according to the flesh, because the flesh is obsolescent. Goldman's God is Yahweh, yet He is a Yahweh of the past, a "Yahweh trapped in amber." The Yahweh of today is not only the God who was born as the child promised in Eden, but the Man who never married or had children. The blessing promised to all nations through Abraham was not the merely the removal of the curse upon the Land and the womb (territory and offspring) but the removal of the fear of death in the promise of resurrection. These blessings were all poured out in Christ.

How then do we interpret Israel's stubborn refusal to disappear? Goldman notes that while the Arab Spring will become a Winter (demographically-speaking) within one generation, Israel currently has the only increasing birthrate in the entire Middle East.

America is no longer the future, but the preservation of Israel is most definitely a testimony to something historical, not a glimpse of the way forward. Judaism serves as an antidote to gnosticism for Christianity, a miraculous testimony like the body of Lot's wife a white, leprous memorial to a judgment *in the past.* Israel exists only because she is protected by the once dominant Christian nations who drew her under their wings. She too must eventually succumb to the Gospel of Christ or return to the dust.

Flesh is not transcendent. Flesh was designed to be transcended by fire. Israel, and indeed America, will be transcended. All God's darlings end up on the altar. The promised child—whether it be European Christendom, the American vision, or the hope of Israel—is ever offered on Mount Moriah for the sake of greater promises.

There is no eternal people. All nations are destined for a larger melting pot, a hotter fire. Every tribe, every circumcision, every culture, every nation, every tongue, every familial baptism, every distinction founded on the old birth, is doomed. Hidden in every cultural and lingual extinction, every brutal war, every abundance, every natural disaster, every economic collapse, every trade agreement, every technological advancement, is the leaven of the Gospel. The yeast that continues to consume and assimilate every other culture, every blood, ancient or modern, is the fire from the unseen mountain, the Spirit of Christ. Here, at last, is the eternal people.

COVENANT

"IT TAKES ON FORM
LIKE CLAY
UNDER A SEAL..."
(JOB 38:14)

6

IMAGES OF GOD

THEANDRIC PLENIPOTENTIARY ITERATION

Typology is the science of recognizing the shape of one thing stamped upon, or into, something else. This is not an exact science by any means, and is thus prone to abuse.

Thankfully, the Bible does not give us isolated "indentations" to interpret; it gives them to us in *sequences*. Sequences of ideas, like sequences of musical notes, are much easier to recognize, even if our identification of them is not yet as refined as it needs to be.

THEANDROS

Every sequence is a retelling of the Covenant story using different images. The same Divine thoughts or actions take on "flesh" (matter) in many different ways.

59

Typology is "theandric" (my new favorite word). It is the acting of the Spirit of God upon matter to form it into "language." Theandric literally combines God and Man, but Tabernacle, Temple and Cosmos are all macrocosmic *human* houses. God impresses Himself upon Mankind as heaven impresses itself upon earth, and Man impresses himself upon Woman (1 Corinthians 11:7). The goal is *reproduction.*

Earth gradually takes on the image, the glory, of heaven. In fact, the glory of earth will be greater than the glory of heaven, as the Bride's glory is the "exposition" of the sweet riddles of the Bridegroom. The postmillennial glory of the Gospel will not just be the denouement of the imagined glory of heaven, but of a glory *greater* than heaven, the future glory of the earth revealed by the Spirit (1 Corinthians 2:9-10).

> And this one *(Initiation)*
>   hath called unto that, *(Delegation)*
>   and hath said: *(Presentation)*
>   'Holy, Holy, Holy, *(Purification)*
>   is Jehovah of Hosts, *(Transformation)*
>   The fullness of all the [Land] *(Vindication)*
> is His glory.' *(Representation)*
> (Isaiah 6:3, Young's Literal Translation)

Finally face to face, all veils removed, the first speech of the new era will be the first speech of the old, with one addition, a Pentecostal one:

Jasper cylinder seal and modern clay impression: monstrous lions and lion-headed eagles, Mesopotamia, Uruk Period (4100 BC–3000 BC). Louvre Museum

SWEET COUNSEL

This is now *(Sabbath)*
  bone of my bones *(Passover)*
    flesh of my flesh *(Firstfruits)*
      And Spirit of my Spirit *(Pentecost)*
    She shall be called Woman, *(Trumpets)*
  Because out of Man *(Atonement)*
she was taken. *(Booths - Ingathering)*
(Genesis 2:23, with center line added)

As mentioned above, the word "theandric" is a combination of *theos* and *andros,* God and man. God's image is stamped upon man physically, and then ethically. *Theandros* is the God-man. God breathed physical life into Adam, but Adam forfeited the ethical image, his "Pentecost," at the Fall. His reception of God's ethical life (and true abundance) was postponed until after the Ascension of the first *ethical* Man as representative. The curses upon Land and womb were physical reminders of Adam's spiritual sterility. He heard the Law but there were no fruits of the Spirit. The word of life was spoken but Adam was hard, red clay.

PLENIPOTENCE

My second-favorite word is plenipotentiary. It denotes somebody who has the full authority of their master. Plenty (full) and potent (power) give you the idea. A perfect example is Joseph, son of Jacob. He was given the full authority of his father over his brothers. Then he was given the full authority of Potiphar. Finally, he received the ring, or seal, of Pharaoh.

Before telegraph, telegrams, telephones and emails, trusted ambassadors needed the power to negotiate with allies and enemies without immediate recourse to their masters. Plenipotence does not simply represent the *words* of the master (the "letter of the law") in obedient acts, but the very *mind* of the master, in wise judgments. The thoughts and plans of the master were revealed to trustworthy confidants and counselors.

> No longer do I call you servants, for the servant does not know what his master is doing; but I have called you friends, for all that I have heard from my Father I have made known to you. (John 15:15)

In effect, the ambassador *was* his master's living image, a representative with whom interaction was regarded as equivalent to correspondence with the master, since the ambassador not only carried the explicit letter of the law but understood its implicit "spirit," its intended outcomes. This also means that rejection of the ambassador was a rejection of the kingdom of the master.

> So Jesus said to them, "Truly, truly, I say to you, the Son can do nothing of his own accord, but only what he sees the Father doing. For whatever the Father does, that the Son does likewise." (John 5:19)

When the Jewish leaders "blasphemed" the Spirit of God, they were hard, red clay, material which would not be shaped by the potter: vessels for destruction.

Then you shall break the flask in the sight of the men who go with you, and shall say to them, "Thus says the Lord of hosts: So will I break this people and this city, as one breaks a potter's vessel, so that it can never be mended." (Jeremiah 19:10-11)

ITERATION

Iteration is the "fractal" abundance of the Creation. As God used fractals in Creation to produce abundant beauty and variety from simple formulae, so He does through His Son in the Church. Iteration is the repetition of an image, although it does not require that each repetition be identical. This is not simple addition, but multiplication and expansion; it is not simply growth but an increase in complexity and glory.

The Son of God brought the engraved image of the law to life in flesh, He died, and His tomb was sealed by the Jewish and Roman authorities, representing the entire world. It was an attempt to maintain the old order, the integrity of the Old Covenant and its Law. Case closed. But the Old Covenant was designed to die, to be completed, to be opened, in the New.

When the stone was removed, the seal was broken, and so were the authorities which it represented. What was bound on earth was bound in heaven. Likewise, what was now loosed on earth would be loosed in heaven. When Jesus rose from the dead, He broke the seal placed by the Law on the tomb of every believer. This brings us to the seals in the book of Revelation.

The Revelation is structured after Israel's journey from Egypt to Canaan. Jesus' ascension to heaven in chapters 4-5 corresponds to Moses' ascension of Sinai. However, Jesus does not hold clay tablets but a scroll with seven seals. Moses began the process and Jesus was ending it. The pattern stamped into Christ, as pliable as clay or wax, graven into His head, feet, hands and side, was a seal of authority. Jesus sat not in the seat of Moses with the power of death, as did the Pharisees, but on a throne with even greater authority, the power of eternal life. The sealed scroll was not a Law but a title deed, a will, a testament, the legal inheritance of every believer.

Like Joseph, who was the "image" of Pharaoh, Jesus was faithful and had been given all power. This pattern was about to be opened and repeated, by the Spirit, in the saints. Now, in a new body, the Church, He was coming to take possession of all nations.

As the seals were broken, the saints of the Firstfruits Church were "sealed" as little scrolls, ambassadors of the Covenant, representatives of Christ invested by the Spirit with all His authority and the full power of independent action on His behalf.

Thus, the seal on each saint speaks not only of ownership; it speaks of *mission*. Each saint was an image of Jesus, and as a body, the Bridal glory of Jesus. They were flesh on the bones of Joseph. As plenipotentiaries for Jesus, the apostles were living epistles, bearing His marks, His stamp, in their bodies.

SWEET COUNSEL

In Revelation, the final apostle John digests a little book and speaks the last legal words over Jerusalem, with all the authority of his Master. The roles once held by angels are now held by Spirit-filled men.

Just as Jesus opened the scroll and rode the White Horse of the Gospel through the Spirit of Pentecost, so the seals on the saints were broken in their martyrdom. Once ascended, they rode with Him upon White Horses to bring judgment upon those who would not believe their report.

Jesus imaged God perfectly. The story of all previous covenants was rolled out in, stamped upon, His life and ministry. After His ascension, that obedient, bloody pattern was rolled out upon the Land. With this understanding of the ways of God, the words of Paul become all the more severe and good. His two-edged sword is sharp, bared, and swinging death-and-resurrection *to and fro* like a sickle throughout the empire. His very words reiterate the pattern of Creation, Sacrifice, Law, Promises, Feasts and Dominion.

TRANSCENDENCE

In him we have obtained an inheritance,
(Creation: Sabbath – Genesis – Initiation)

HIERARCHY

having been predestined according to the
purpose of him who works all things according
to the counsel of his will,
(Division: Passover – Exodus – Delegation)

ETHICS

so that we who were the first to hope in
Christ might be to the praise of his glory.
(Ascension: Firstfruits – Leviticus – Presentation)

In him you also, when you heard the word
of truth, the gospel of your salvation,
(Testing: Pentecost – Numbers – Purification)

and believed in him, were sealed with the
promised Holy Spirit,
(Maturity: Trumpets – Deuteronomy – Transformation)

OATH/SANCTIONS

who is the guarantee of our inheritance until
we acquire possession of it,
(Conquest: Atonement – Joshua – Vindication)

SUCCESSION

to the praise of his glory.
(Glorification: Booths – Judges – Representation)

(Ephesians 1:11-14)

SWEET COUNSEL

The seal of the Spirit is not something to "keep me safe until heaven." If I fail to live publicly for Christ, I remain a Covenant document with an unbroken seal, a message whose contents were intended by God to be sounded as Trumpets and poured out as Bowls, my testimony remains a sealed tomb.

If you are sealed, you have a mission. You will be ridiculed and hated, but you will be vindicated upon those who remain enemies of God. Jesus was, and so were the apostles. The Gospel will continue to be preached until the glory of the earth not only rivals but surpasses the glory of heaven. Heaven has a singular glory. Earth multiplies, vindicates, the glory of God.

"Our heaven is up yonder with God.
God's heaven is down here upon earth
with us. His delights are
with the sons of men."
– Andrew Bonar

THE FRUITFUL
LIFE IS A LIFE
THAT IS
CONSTANTLY
BEING
BEHEADED
BY THE TRUTH.

7
SIMPLY IRRESISTIBLE

LEGALISM AND LEADERSHIP

You may have had some experience with a "legalistic" church or Christian. A domineering leadership is a curse to the work of God, but so many people who make the decision to leave such ministries or individuals behind become "lawless" in their liberty. They swap one problem for another. What is really going on there, and what is the *Bible's* solution for legalism?

As usual, the answer can be found in the primeval events of Genesis 1-3. The pattern of Adam's *Testing* is the foundation for all of history. The intention of God was for a simple external Law to become an internal guiding principle: submission to God leads to authority over the world. Adam was to achieve a basic level of *self*-government, of *self*-legislation. He was to meditate on God's Law, digest it, and expound upon it when challenged. As a leader, he was to govern those in his care with wisdom, that is, he was to make his own mini-laws based upon what he had learned from God's inspired Law. God told Adam not to eat of the Tree of Knowledge. It appears that Adam had prohibited Eve from even *touching* it.

If Adam had repeated the Law when the serpent began his slander of God, it would have proved that the external Law, the "elemental principles" *(stoicheia)* had found a home in him. For Eve, the Law of God would now be embodied, incarnated, in Adam's faith, and the Word of God would now be the *Government* of Adam.

We see the same thing in Christ. He finished the "elemental" Mosaic Law by obeying it to the letter. It is now no longer the Law of Moses but the Law of Christ. And it is the Law of liberty because He makes *us* self-governing by His Spirit.

THE NATURE OF SPIRITUAL LEADERSHIP

This brings us to the nature of spiritual leadership. *Stoicheian* Law is legal, but not relational. It is an external force, a coercion. The Law is good but it is powerless to affect real change. It is just a safety rail.

So, Jesus sent us His Spirit to make *relational* what was previously only *legal*. Why, then, do *Christian* leaders with good intentions sometimes become legalistic bullies? Because relational isn't enough. Truly spiritual leadership is *irresistible*.

Adam had been given the Law. He had legal responsibilities. He was married to Eve. Now he was a relational being. But if he had stepped in to rescue Eve from the serpent, Eve would have found Adam simply irresistible. Through self-sacrifice, he would have proven his love, not only for God, but for Eve. And the willing self-sacrifice of the Head brings the purifying fire of love to the entire Body.

Christian leadership, and indeed, any Christian witness, is not to be simply *relational*. It is to be *irresistible,* that is, self-sacrificial. Douglas Wilson has illustrated this principle in many ways concerning family relationships. If a husband or father has "enough in the emotional bank accounts" of his wife and children, they will submit to his requirements as he images God to them.

If a leader has to *tell* you he is the leader, he is not leading by the Spirit. It is coercion. When leaders are self-exalting instead of being self-sacrificial, they become manipulative. They do this by using their God-given role as legislators (writers of mini-laws) as a means of control rather than a means of protection and training. Instead of being advocates like Jesus they become accusers, *satans.* Their domain becomes elitist, inward-looking instead of outward looking.

So, according to Jesus, how are we to disciple the nations? Our witness, like Jesus, is a combination of the Word and flesh. It is the Law lived out in a life. There will still be times when hands-on disciplinary action is required, as we see with the disciples, but overall they found Jesus simply irresistible. They knew He loved them and would die for them. As Paul puts it, His love *constrained* them (2 Corinthians 5:14). He could make demands because their bank accounts were full of His grace. And, since His death and resurrection, so are ours. We, like they, understand His heart. Now we are willing to die *for Him.*

God loves Laws. We know this because He wrote all the good ones. Adam, too, was to become a lawgiver, a legislator, a judge, a representative of his Father. But this was to be sourced in his own acts of *self*-government. His obedience would have brought freedom for all of us.

This exposes the self-delusion of legalism. The Pharisees were a brood of vipers (offspring of the serpent) who used the *stoicheia* to assert their own authority rather than to demonstrate the goodness of God. The Law became a cover for their own *lack* of submission to God. Instead of putting themselves *under* God's Law, they put themselves *over* it.

This failure of self-legislation meant that their "righteousness" was a hypocritical tyranny. Instead of exemplary submission to the Law bringing freedom for those in their care, Law became a means of control. Instead of multiplied "fruits" of righteousness, they produced a plethora of superstitious rules. The Pharisees wrote laws which were "right in their own eyes," not God's. They became so concerned about

Herod (Hérode) (1886-1894)
James Tissot

attending to the minor details of arbitrary man-made rules that these clouds of little legalisms were used to obscure their very real God-given responsibilities.

This sad process is very apparent in modern Western Culture. The rulers reject God's Law and their people become undisciplined children whose every move must be guided by legislation. Instead of the Ten Laws which bring freedom and prosperity, we are bound by thousands which retard it.

The only way to exceed such "righteousness" is to internalize the Law. And the only way to internalize the Law is to submit the flesh to it. If I submit, as Adam should have, or die, as Jesus did, my spirit becomes irresistible, and gathers the Bride from the nations. When Adam "dies," Eve can't resist Him. In some sense, my obedience multiplies "my spirit" just as Jesus' obedience sent His Spirit. My submission to God begets submission to God in others.

The Pharisees misunderstood the liberty of Jesus and His disciples because He was *self*-legislating. He—with the disciples in tow—could pass right through their little legalistic walls like a resurrected Body, a new kind of Tabernacle. They could not bind Him because He was already bound—from the inside. One who is self-legislating under God marches to the beat of a different drum, and it is a beat that the Spirit-called human heart finds irresistible.

So, the cure for legalism is not libertarianism. One of A. W. Tozer's mottos was "Others may; I cannot."

When it came to himself, Tozer was a total legalist. When it came to others, he was a libertarian. This is the same as the biblical process of "binding and loosing."[1] A willing leader is bound that his people might be freed.

Jesus was bound that I might be loosed. Now I have freedom, but it is found in being bound for others, paying it forward. This means that my actions will rarely be consistent with the hard-and-fast rules of the world. My law will be the Law of Christ, the Law of the Spirit. It means I will be consistently lawful but infinitely flexible.

The abundance of the "abundant life" is *other people,* a harvest that comes from being a seed that is willing to die. It is an authority bestowed by God resulting from a growing humility. The fruitful life is a life that is constantly being beheaded by the truth.

If you are a Christian, you know the pain of this constant pruning. It is the perfect marriage of Law and Grace. God never disciplines us merely for our own sakes. It is not about us, and in that sense our discipline isn't even about Him. He is always thinking of others. That is what makes our New Adam so irresistible. Jesus does not coerce His disciples, and yet His kingdom grows.

---

1   See the discussion in "Binding and Loosing" in *God's Kitchen: Theology You Can Eat & Drink,* 125.

GOD CANNOT
BE SEPARATED
FROM EITHER
HIS ATTRIBUTES
OR HIS GIFTS.
TO HAVE A
GOD-GIVEN
INTERNAL MORAL
COMPASS IS TO
HAVE GOD HIMSELF.

8
INTERNAL LAW

GOVERNMENT UPON
HIS SHOULDERS

Maturation is the process of making God's "external law" into our internal law, as our operating, animating principle. This has huge implications for sanctification, but it also explains a lot of what is going on in the Bible's symbolism and architecture.

The test in Eden was not two dimensional. The deceit by Satan was not allowed by God simply to demonstrate whether Adam was "in" or "out." The question was not, "Are you on my side or not?" As Douglas Wilson notes, when he was sent by his father to the cellar for misbehavior, it was not because he wasn't a Wilson. It was because he *was* a Wilson.

A father disciplines his child out of love, with one eye on the future. All of God's judgments are "visionary justice." This is where the process of atonement comes in. It cuts off the past and frees the future.

What is the third dimension of testing? Enlargement. Heaven was created "solid state," but every part of the earth was designed to grow to maturity. If Adam had obeyed, it would not mean he had earned greater authority but that he had grown, been enlarged, to shoulder such government. We see the same process in the lives of all of the patriarchs, especially Joseph. Continued faithfulness, despite betrayal and hardship, meant that wisdom developed and he could be exalted in one fell swoop to rule the world—and call his brothers to the table.

The difference between Man and the rest of creation is self-awareness. Under heaven's eye, the human is both the observed *and* the observer. Man, unlike animals, requires not only a diet of food but also a steady diet of truth. Spiritual growth begins with hearing the truth, and hearing presumes a relationship. This is where faith comes in. Faith is *relational,* resulting in works carried out in response to the speaker of truth. Much of the discussion concerning "faith and works" fails to consider growth and relationship as parts of the equation.

True works are not meritorious, but are the evidence of faith, even in the life of Jesus. James Jordan writes:

> The problem with the "covenant of works" notion lies in the fact that it is linked up with merit theology. There is no merit theology in the Bible. Merit theology is a hangover of medieval Roman Catholicism.
> The problem with much "active and passive" talk

is that it is part of the same erroneous scheme: Jesus' "active obedience" earned merits that are then given to me, merits that Adam was supposed to earn. Such "merits" are some kind of "works," and though this is not said, what is implied are something like Herculean labors, something beyond merely remaining faithful.

But that's not what happened. Jesus simply remained faithful. He did not do any heroic works— there is no heroism in the gospel anywhere; only faithfulness. In a large sense, all of Jesus' "work" was "passive." He did not "go beyond" mere faithful obedience to the Law. But as a result of doing just that and no more, He matured into full adulthood. Notice that He was proclaimed king when He arrived at Jerusalem, was tried as a king, was robed as a king, and was crucified as a king. Contrary to Presbyterian theology, Jesus did not die primarily as a priest but as Melchizedek, as a king. That is, as an adult.

Or, better, as the One who was on the brink of becoming king, as the anointed Prince. Passing through death on the tree and then being resurrected in a transfigured state, Jesus became fully King and Adult.

Jesus resisted Satan in the wilderness. That's what Adam failed to do. From that point on, for three plus years, He matured in faith, beyond the point where Adam failed. He matured to the point of being ready for adult responsibilities. Through His death, he became fully mature and was given dominion over all nations, over the wider world into which Adam had been prematurely cast.

That is the point of Galatians 3-4. Formerly we were children, but now in union with Jesus Christ we have become adults. What we have received from Jesus is not a collection of "merits," but rather His maturity.[1]

So, faithful works are not meritorious, but neither are unfaithful works. The difference between the good works of a Christian and the good works of a Muslim is *true relationship with God*. Works without faith are not relational. Without faith it is impossible to please God. A son who despises his father and does his chores merely for his own benefit will be disowned. In essence, God gave Adam one law. Adam whined and asked "Why?" And God said, "Because I am your father." It was not a test of obedience but a test of relationship. Law and love are not the same, but they cannot be separated. Internal law is not only "loving the standard" as something that brings life, but growing through a perception of the goodness of the law, and beyond it, to a love for the Lawgiver and an expression of that love to others.

External law is Man under government, under the sword. But internal law is not merely Man *in* government, bearing the sword as a wise ruler. It is man "with God." Maturity is an increase in authority due to a

---

[1] James B. Jordan, quoted in an online discussion. For detailed discussion see James B. Jordan, "Merit Versus Maturity: What Did Jesus Do For Us?" in *The Federal Vision*, eds. Steve Wilkins and Duane Gardner.

growth in relationship. This is because God cannot be separated from either His attributes or His gifts.

To have a God-given internal moral compass is to have God Himself. To have internal law is to have Christ Himself in you. Law and love were designed to be married, to be dance partners. Like male and female, neither makes sense without the other. To love God's law is to love God Himself.

So, righteousness is impossible without faith because true humanity is life lived in relation to God. The righteousness of the Pharisees was not righteousness but a power grab. It was law operating without love, which is vengeance and not mercy, the religion of Cain, Lamech and the Herods. Rather than being the image and bearer of *God's* standard, Man makes *himself* into the Lawgiver, the ultimate source of authority. But Man's law is only two dimensional. Bereft of love, human rulers are only concerned with compliance, not growth. Unfeigned love for a ruler is rare. Human rulers have subjects, not sons.

But Jesus did not atone for our sins merely to right a wrong. Destroying us would accomplish that. He was sent to us by the Father to reconcile us to Him. Jesus told the Pharisees who their real father was: the devil, the one who, beginning in Eden, used the good Law as an instrument of death. Satan's "sons" abused the Law in this way in the account of the woman caught in adultery.

Jesus' story of the Pharisee and the tax collector is not about pride, but about pride as a hindrance to reconciliation. The unfaithful *"righteousness"* of the Pharisee blinded him to the truth. The "faithful" *unrighteousness* of the tax collector allowed God to open his eyes. The difference was true relationship. The tax collector loved God, and like Joseph, realized that sin was primarily a personal offense against one's Creator (Genesis 39:9). Faith leads to obedience, which leads to understanding. Promise leads to fulfillment. Thus, faith (promise) leads to sight (fulfillment). This means that growing in godliness is a growth in *vision*. Spiritual growth is first and foremost a developing "judicial maturity," and this is achieved through obedience to the truth. As we obey, more and more we see evil for what it is (especially in ourselves) and it repels us.

The Lord's table is a public demonstration of this. We examine our hearts and die under the Law. We "confess" our sins legally before God because *we see them as they are,* with eyes opened by that Law. But with those eyes *we also see Jesus as He is,* and "confess" Him as our legal advocate. We leave the assembly reconciled, resurrected, with the gift of eternal life in the Spirit.

We do see this exact pattern of Law and Spirit, forming and filling, all through the Bible. It is the heart of the "Bible Matrix."[2] Obedience brings greater authority, and disobedience means we lose even what we have—because we can't be trusted with it as stewards.

---

2   This is discussed at length in *Bible Matrix II: The Covenant Key.*

The Transfiguration of Christ (1455)
Giovanni Bellini

> For to everyone who has will more be given, and he
> will have an abundance. But from the one who has
> not, even what he has will be taken away.
> (Matthew 25:29)

This process also reveals the heart of God. The Law gives form to life but its intended end is always relational, that is, fellowship, a blessed unity of mind, with the resulting kindred spirit. Communion is the result of reconciliation, thus only possible through repentance and faith.

Jesus' obedience gave us the Spirit, and all of the riches of His "judicially mature" Adamic mind. The "glorious future" is when we are "gods," that is, *elohim*, judges, perfect physical images and perfect ethical (legal) representatives of the Father. Every Covenant is an opportunity to image God in the world as creator, protector and provider. Every Covenant is an opportunity not only to demonstrate, but to become "the righteousness of God" (2 Corinthians 5:21), extensions of His mind and character in the way Moses' helpers extended his judicial ministry.

The way in which we "judge" (assess) sin has a direct bearing on the preciousness of Christ to us. As we grow, we judge Him to be more and more righteous, and this transforms us into His image. The Spirit opens our eyes to behold Him in His beauty, both the beauty of His Law and the beauty of His grace, and this changes us. Like Adam, our eyes are opened, and we are clothed, covered.

As our spiritual (obedient) life progresses, so does the opening of our eyes. The light of the Spirit becomes not something descending upon us but emanating from within us. God makes us into Tabernacles.

This is what we see at Jesus' Transfiguration. Though the cloud was present, the three tabernacles proposed by Peter were not required. Jesus needed no tent because He was now the Tent. The Shekinah within the tent and Temple was always a gift from God once His instructions had been obeyed. Robert Ervin Hough gives us a beautiful description of this process:

> Christ has two glories. There is the glory which He had with the Father before the foundation of the world (John 17:5), which is His inherent glory, a glory which cannot be added to nor taken from. As the Redeemer of mankind He has an acquired glory, the glory which belongs to Him as the Saviour. As the Son of God He came in the glory of the Father, but as the Son of man He will come in His own glory in which His own people will share (John 17:22). The Transfiguration was the foreshadowing of His acquired glory, the glory which the three disciples were permitted to see on the mount.
>
> There were a number of occurrences in connection with the Transfiguration which did much to prepare the disciples to understand and appreciate the Divine purpose in the tragic events of the closing period of the Savior's life in the flesh.
>
> First, there was the Transfiguration. It was an

undeniable confirmation of the pronouncement of Peter concerning the person of Christ and the pledge of His final and complete victory. In the mount all the prophetic words concerning the Messiah were made surer to human understanding. The Transfiguration involved a radical change in the physical appearance of Christ. It was not a transformation wrought from without but a change which originated from within. It may be considered in some respects the counterpart of the incarnation. In the incarnation His Deity was veiled in flesh (Phil. 2:5-8), while at the Transfiguration the veil of the flesh became transparent so that His true character and dignity might be observed for a brief period.

At the Transfiguration Christ reached the climax of His human life. He had failed in nothing, for He had met every temptation and defeated every tempter in every encounter. Having fulfilled every demand of the Father's will there was no need for Him to die personally. He might have returned to heaven with Moses and Elijah, to take His place with the Father from when He had come.[3]

The legal testimony of two witnesses, Moses (external law – elements [stoicheia] hidden in the earth) and Elijah (internal law – hidden in heaven), corroborated in the court of the Father, and Jesus was vindicated as God-Man. Moses and Elijah were then put into Jesus to be taken into the grave and fulfilled. Many believe they

---

3   Robert Ervin Hough, *The Ministry of the Glory Cloud*, 83-84.

were the two men testifying at the ascension. In Jesus, they were united as a new law, the Law of Christ, which was conferred *upon* the saints in the gift of the Spirit, and revealed *in* them through faithful obedience as glory. Internal law is the gift of the seer, the presence of the One from whose eyes nothing in heaven or on earth is hidden.

> But now the righteousness of God apart from the law is revealed, being witnessed by the Law and the Prophets. (Romans 3:21)

THE PROSPERITY
GOSPEL IS A
SATANIC LIE, YET
TRUE PROSPERITY
WILL ONLY EVER
COME THROUGH
AN APPLICATION
OF THE GOSPEL.

9
CASH AND COVENANT

THIRTY PIECES OF SILVER

The "Bible Matrix" is the shape of Creation but it is also the shape of Covenant. It is the process of promise and fulfillment. We see it in Eden. We see it in Canaan. Every Covenant is a mission, a tour of duty, resulting in a safe place to live, a home of abundance, peace and glory. It should be no surprise that it is also the process that underpins true economic growth.

Capitalism is based on the biblical Covenant structure. Good businessmen understand how it works. It invariably necessitates the risk and sacrifice of what we now possess in the hope of a greater reward. Steve Jobs told us that, and demonstrated it again and again. It takes money to make money. This requires faith in the one who made the promise, even though business people do not recognize that the source of their abundance is the hand of God.

God calls Man to work, which involves risk (faith), a sacrifice and some obedience to laws (which include natural and business laws), which will bring fulfillment of the promise—a greater abundance than what you sacrificed. That is where capitalism ends, but it is not where *Covenant* ends, and here is the problem for which Socialism is tendered as a solution.

The final step of Covenant is that *you*, the risk taker, become a shelter, a house, for the helpless. The final step is *generosity*. Capitalism, or the "free market," only works in a moral society. This is why the shape of good economics resembles the shape of the work in history of the Gospel. Jesus gave His life to gain abundant life for us all. He believed in the promise made to Him by the Father, the promise of resurrection—a new body. His poverty was not something to be embraced eternally. It was an investment in the future.

Christian Socialists forget that Jesus now owns everything. All the great saints were rich people who risked their wealth for even greater wealth, a wealth that included a legacy of other people—*a household*. The "glory that was set before Him" was also the glory of the Church, a new body that includes every believer. Jesus Himself is our covering. We are only saved because of His atonement, His "covering." He, the king of kings, the great Land Lord, is our shelter.

But His kingdom is also growing to become a great tree, a shelter for the nations. As Western culture cuts itself free from the constraints of God, it also cuts itself

Detail from *The Capture of Christ*
Cimabue

off from the abundance which results from the working of His Spirit. The spiritual decline has led to moral decline which in turn has led to demographic and economic decline. And what is our response? Do we turn back to God? No. We attempt to minimize the risk. We don't want the safety of the "shelter" promised by God and available through risk and sacrifice. We want to keep what we have now and spread it as thinly and as fairly as possible. That is what Socialism is, and it is exactly the temptation offered to Adam in Eden and Jesus in the wilderness. It is a counterfeit kingdom at the hand of Satan. It involves no risk, no faith, and thus no growth. It is a bubble. Worse, it is idolatry. The nanny state is a satanic security, a corporate Judas, where the voters, in their President, crucify Jesus with a kiss. Their loyalty to God as Creator, Lawmaker and Provider exists only in lip service.

So much for the political Left, but those on the political Right also have a misplaced faith. They believe that Capitalism *per se*, the free market, is their savior. But Capitalism itself has no moral constraints. It is the godly Covenant process cut off from God. It is those whom God has put in authority (and whom He deliberately made wealthy) using their position for their own gain, which is why Jesus saved His sharpest words for the Jewish leaders. The rich get richer and the poor get poorer (leaving out for a moment the hardworking middle class who actually produce stuff and support everyone). The opportunity that comes with biblical economics is removed from the reach of those at the bottom. We will always have the poor with us, for numerous reasons, but a society with a growing rank of "helpless" reveals a fundamental problem. A Christian culture is a culture of opportunity because it is a culture that flows from Covenant.

To sum up, Capitalism without God knows little about generosity. The Socialists do see the problem, but they do not replace the greed with generosity. They fill the God-gap by breaking other commandments. They fill it with envy and theft, and then sit enthroned like Orwell's pigs at the farmer's table. And once the risk is gone, the abundance is gone too.

Based on Church history, I have no doubt that there is even greater prosperity awaiting the world. But like Israel, like Adam, to enter into God's rest, we must turn back to Him in obedient faith. The prosperity gospel is a satanic lie, yet true prosperity will only ever come through an application of the Gospel. We embrace risk and sacrifice for greater blessing at every step.

UNDER THE MINISTRY OF ELISHA, WE HAVE SONS OF ISRAEL DESTROYED BY WILD BEASTS, AND THE WOMBS OF THE WOMEN IN JERICHO, ONCE POISONED BY A WELL, NOW HEALED BY THE PROPHET.

10

I WILL KILL HER CHILDREN WITH DEATH

WHO IS THE REAL JERICHO?

Atheists love to embarrass Christians with a snide reference to the story of Elisha setting two bears upon some helpless children. What nobody, even Christians, seem to get is the "Covenant significance" of all the players in the story, harking back to Moses. The prophets were, after all, God's "repo men."

God often retells history in a new way to make a point. God, the Author of the story, also confers meaning upon things as He goes. So, to make sense of this atrocity, not only must we be able to recognize the *shape of this story* as a familiar object, but also recognize the significance of the *characters and places*.

One approach to dealing with the apparent brutality has been to question the age of these "children." In his

Brazos commentary on the books of Kings, Peter Leithart suggests that these "young lads" were actually interns at the local temple of Baal. Bethel, the location of the massacre, was also the location of one of the golden calves installed by Jeroboam, so it was a center of idolatry. However, despite the fact that this demonstrates guilt on the part of the city, it does not explain why the *children* were slain at Elisha's hand.

The chain of events of which this account is a part concerns offspring. Children are the future. A culture with no children has no future (something which Western culture is about to learn). Offspring died when Israel left Egypt, and offspring died when Israel arrived in Canaan. And we should remember that the firstborn of Egypt died to avenge the slaughter of Hebrew infants by Pharaoh eighty years earlier.

When Israel entered the Land, all her male offspring born in the wilderness over the past four decades were circumcised, that is, symbolically "cut off," genealogically speaking. This had to happen before Israel offered Jericho as a whole burnt offering, a firstfruits, to God. All flesh was destroyed, including the infants (another fact that ignorant atheists like to hurl at us).

Here in Kings, however, there is a reversal. Under the ministry of Elisha, we have sons of *Israel* destroyed by wild beasts, and the wombs of the women in *Jericho,* once poisoned by a well, now healed by the prophet. What could this turnabout mean?

The point is that ultimately God is no respecter of

The Children are Slain for Mocking Elisha.
Picture from The Holy Scriptures, Old and New Testaments,
Stuttgart, 1885. Drawings by Gustave Doré

persons. Believing Gentiles (which is what Abraham was prior to his circumcision) would have their place in history, and unbelieving Israelites would be cut off.

Moreover, the two beasts in this event prefigure the devouring of Israel and Judah by Assyria and Babylon. The structure of the passage follows the architecture of the Tabernacle, which puts the word of the prophet in the place of the Ark of the Covenant, on the move out in the field, and the two bears as its flanking cherubim, the two witnesses. It is an earthly version of the flaming chariot of God, carried by heavenly beasts, executing the curses upon those who have broken the Covenant and blessing those, like Rahab, who have believed. This story is a re-enactment of the family histories of the sons of Judah, Perez and Zerah.[1]

It also prefigures the final cutting off in AD66-70: Jerusalem encircled by a Roman ditch and wall (circumcised), her children cut off, as Jesus predicted, and all her genealogical records destroyed with the burning of the Temple. This was, in part, a judgment upon the Herods for the massacre of the infants by Herod the Great, but the judgment itself was brought down by their murder of the apostles and prophets, the

---

[1] Rahab married into the Messianic line, which was at that time carried in the lineage two brothers, Perez and Zerah. Rahab, the prostitute from Jericho, married into the line of Perez, and the line of Zerah was cut off in Achan, who took plunder from Jericho. He was executed along with all his children. A believing Gentile brought children to Israel, and an unbelieving Jew was cut off. See Joshua 22:20; Matthew 1:3-6.

true sons of God. Judaism had become not only a new Jericho, but also a great Jezebel, and Jesus warned the Gentile churches against the same sins:

> Behold, I will throw her onto a sickbed, and those who commit adultery with her I will throw into great tribulation, unless they repent of her works, and I will strike her children dead. And all the churches will know that I am he who searches mind and heart, and I will give to each of you according to your works. (Revelation 2:22-23)

Jesus was simply reiterating the curses of the Mosaic Covenant against those who would take the name of the Lord upon themselves (swear the Covenant oath) in vain. Under Joshua, the Lord would slowly drive the beasts from the Land. If He did it too suddenly, the Land would become desolate (Exodus 23:29). But if the children of Israel were disobedient, this slow victory would be *reversed:*

> And I will let loose the wild beasts against you, which shall bereave you of your children and destroy your livestock and make you few in number, so that your roads shall be deserted. (Leviticus 26:22)

The bears *and* the children have a Covenantal significance conferred upon them in the Torah. You can analyze the bears; you can do an autopsy on the children, but the Bible will not open itself to the minds of rebels. It is one thing for atheists to be ignorant of the Bible, but quite another for Christians.

BIBL ICAL THEO LOGY

THE COVENANT
IS NO LONGER
ADMINISTERED
BY SERVANTS
BUT BY SONS.

11
BETTER ANGELS

SONS OF GOD AND MAN

"Of the angels he says,
'He makes his angels winds
and his ministers a flame of fire.'"
(Hebrews 1:7)

The letters in Revelation are not written to the Churches, but to the pastor of each Church. Quite unexpectedly, Jesus uses the word "angel" to describe each pastor. This is unexpected, and yet, with hindsight, we can see it is something we should have expected all along.

God is the source of all things, and He identifies Himself as such in His speeches. Every speech is Covenantal, and every preamble within His speeches is a statement of *Transcendence*. "I am the Lord your God."

The initial call is followed by delegation, Covenantal *Hierarchy*. A man—an Abraham, a Moses—receives the Word with meekness, and becomes a citizen of heaven, a model for those under his God-given authority and in his care. But such servants were not the first servants of God. Angels were.

SERVANTS, SWORDS AND SONS

We know that angels are God's messengers, the sent ones. They mediated between heaven and earth, and administered the Old Covenant (Acts 7:53, Galatians 3:19, Hebrews 2:2). As mediators of the Law, they served as our tutors. The angel-serpent, a hybrid between heaven and earth, was thus the first false teacher. He was the first corrupt ambassador, or, if you will, the first publican, a "servant-on-the-take," seeking to seize the inheritance promised to Man. A perfect pop-culture illustration of this is the crafty, murderous but eventually doomed butler in Walt Disney's *The Aristocats*. The servant, the messenger, wished to inherit like the son he would never be.

With the coming of the Holy Spirit, the ministry of the angels was complete. Indeed, Revelation 4 shows them casting down their crowns, completing their vows just like the Nazirites did, the holy warriors who offered up their glorious "crowns" of hair as a sacrifice to their Captain. Since Pentecost, the angels of God, the ministers who are a "flame of fire," are now *human* servants. Yet they are not merely servants, but sons who will inherit. With this in mind, something very interesting comes to light concerning the ministry of the angels in the Covenant process. Their ministry never lasted beyond the opening of the Law.

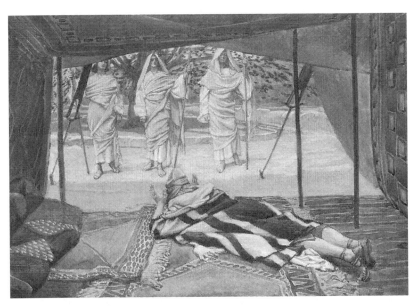

Abraham and the Three Angels (c. 1896-1902)
James Tissot

SWEET COUNSEL

Bible history follows the Covenant pattern. After *Hierarchy* comes *Ethics,* the rules of engagement, the laws for success.

Because the Ethics become a threefold process (the Law is given, opened and received), the fivefold pattern becomes sevenfold, recapitulating the Creation Week, recreating the world in the rite of sacrifice.

TRANSCENDENCE
Initiation (The Call)
Animal chosen *(Day 1: Sabbath)*

HIERARCHY
Delegation (Setting Apart)
Animal cut *(Day 2: Passover)*

ETHICS
Presentation (Promise: External Law)
Flesh lifted up as a nearbringing
(Day 3: Firstfruits - LAW GIVEN)

Purification (Internal Inspection)
Holy fire descends
(Day 4: Pentecost - LAW OPENED)

Transformation (Internal Law)
Fragrant smoke as a witness
(Day 5: Trumpets - LAW RECEIVED)

OATH/SANCTIONS
Vindication (Legal Assessment)
The offering is accepted *(Day 6: Atonement)*

SUCCESSION
Representation (Fulfillment: The Commission)
The Abrahamic Land and womb are blessed
(Day 7: Booths)

The "Day 4" of Covenant history was the Day of Pentecost. It was the day when the "sun, moon and stars," the government, was given to men on earth. What was bound or loosed on earth would be bound or loosed in heaven. The interesting factor is the fiery angels in the Old Testament never get beyond step 4 of the sacrificial process. As "legal fire," guardians with a flaming sword put in place to keep corrupted human flesh from the presence of God, their services are not required once Adam is slain and incinerated as a whole burnt offering.

Angels ruled the Old Covenant, so they could only work through steps 1-4. Angels could be

called in heaven, *(Ark of the Testimony)*

sent to earth, *(Veil)*

take on flesh, *(Bronze Altar & Table)*

and speak the law, *(Lampstand)*

but angels could never take that "flesh" back to heaven. Only a son could do that, because only those in the flesh can procreate. To Abraham and his offspring, Jesus was "the Angel of the Lord," a humble servant. For Jesus to inherit the Adamic promises, to produce from His body a "corporate Eve," a holy humanity, the Son of God had to become the Son of Man.

WOMBS AND TOMBS

The smoke of step 5 pictures the fragrant resurrection body, the Bride. The angelic ministry was thus a three-and-a-half, like the failed ministry of Adam which it temporarily replaced. They were guardians of a divided, prostrate body, the bleeding sacrifice, as Abraham was. They kept the birds and beasts away until the coming of the Spirit who would gather the Bride from Adam's body and "close up the flesh" opened in Circumcision.

Angels could not bring about the true bridal body, the Day 5, except in type. Limited to Days 1 to 4, angels could become incarnate, flesh and blood, but they always ascended in the flames of holy fire. We see this in Judges 13, as the messenger brings about the miraculous birth of a son. One such type was Samson, the holy warrior, a Nazirite from birth. The limited, heraldic ministry of the Old Covenant angels is quite apparent.

> So Manoah took the young goat with the grain offering, and offered it on the rock to the Lord, to the one who works wonders, and Manoah and his wife were watching. And when the flame went up toward heaven from the altar, the angel of the Lord went up in the flame of the altar. Now Manoah and his wife were watching, and they fell on their faces to the ground.
>
> The angel of the Lord appeared no more to Manoah and to his wife. Then Manoah knew that he was the angel of the Lord. (Judges 13:19-21)

We can also observe this limitation in Genesis 19, where the holy fire falling upon Sodom brings barrenness to Lot's wife but conception to Sarah. We do not hear about the angels after the fire falls. Where did they go? We can safely assume that, as ministers of fire, they ascended in the fire as did Manoah's angel.

Angels could announce new life from the womb, and eventually new life from the tomb. They could bring fruitfulness to an Eve, and they could be the Lord's *heavenly* host. But angels could never actually *be* Eve, the resurrection body, a true swarm. They could go before armies of men to bring victory, but only as servants, not as sons. Their ministry always concerned the delivery of the Covenant Head, the "firstborn" promises of fruitfulness made to Adam and to Abraham. This is why the angels are *never* female, and *always* fullgrown.

Likewise, Daniel's friends emerged from the fiery furnace of Nebuchadnezzar but the angel did not. The servant fulfilled his ministry in the flames, but the sons emerged as a witness to God's faithfulness, prefiguring the coming national resurrection of Israel.

> Are they not all ministering spirits sent out to serve for the sake of those who are to inherit salvation? (Hebrews 1:14)

This background helps us to understand the use of the word "angel" in Revelation. The book begins with the identification of the Lord, then the delegation of His authority to "sent ones," the Church pastors called to serve the saints. These New Covenant angels had bodies of flesh, like the Old Covenant ones. But in the Revelation these servants did not end their ministry in the fire. The Firstfruits martyrs were slain and resurrected. In resurrection bodies of flesh, as virgin warriors, a holy bride, it was now *they* who commanded the angels who went before them against God's enemies. And the order was to bring vengeance.

The ministry of the angels never reached beyond they opening of the Law, either in speech or in judgment, Oath or Sanctions. Thus, the last ministry of the Old Covenant angels in the Bible was the pouring out of the curses of the fruitfulness of Abraham and the holiness of Moses, the fire of Sodom and the plagues of Egypt, upon Jerusalem (Revelation 11:8).

This ascension of the Firstfruits Church to receive the kingdom was revealed in Daniel 7. Christ, the Son of Man, the Ancient of Days, was enthroned already as the Covenant Head. His legs were a stream of holy fire that descended to the Land. In response to this ministry of fire, the Body of saints, as "one *like* the Son of Man," rose to meet Him in the air.[1] Unlike the angels, the saints ascended in bodies of flesh and blood. This was the blessed hope of the apostles and the Old Covenant martyrs, the first resurrection.

---

[1]   See James B. Jordan *The Handwriting On The Wall*, 337-340, for an explanation of this interpretation in relation to Leviticus 16.

SWEET COUNSEL

It is no accident that the ministry of the saints is called "ev-*angel*-ism." Ours is not a ministry of heraldry, but a ministry of testimony *after the fact* and resurrection *in the flesh.*

Thus, New Covenant angels are *better* angels. The Covenant is no longer administered by servants but by sons. The Pentecostal fire has been passed on to us in the Law of Love. Like Christ we can be

TRANSCENDENCE
called, *(Ark of the Testimony)*

> **HIERARCHY**
> set apart, *(Veil)*

>> **ETHICS**
>> offer our flesh, *(Bronze Altar & Table)*
>>> speak the truth and die, *(Lampstand)*
>> rise and witness, *(Incense Altar)*

> **OATH/SANCTIONS**
> call down curses upon God's enemies,
> and redemption for His friends *(Co-mediators)*

SUCCESSION
and, most importantly of all, feast with God in heaven, and inherit the earth. *(Rest and Rule)*[2]

---

2   See *God's Kitchen: Theology You Can Eat & Drink,* 315, for the role of angels in the banquet of Covenant history.

DOGS AND PIGS
ARE THE CHURCH
AND THE STATE
"ON THE TAKE."

12
DOGS AND PIGS

Who are the dogs and pigs against whom Jesus warns His hearers in Matthew 7?

Firstly, there are clues in the literary structure, which turns out to be so finely crafted and allusory that it could come only from the mouth of the One who spoke the Creation into existence, and also spoke the words of every subsequent Covenant.

THE STRUCTURE

Splitting the text into single words and simple phrases might seem to be taking things too far. However, since we speak of Covenants being "objective" or "subjective," any sentence containing a subject and object is potentially "Covenantal." Language begins a chain of authority but is itself a chain of authority. Observe the movement from above to beside to below (as appears in the Ten Words) in Jesus' single sentence.

The sentence itself is a "two-level" fractal, with the

117

lights of the Lampstand, as seven pearls, given their own stanza *within* the stanza.

Do not *(ARK – Initiation: Transcendent Imperative)*

give *(VEIL – Delegation)*

that which is holy *(ALTAR – Presentation)*

to the **dogs** *(TABLE – Firstfruits)*

LAMPSTAND – Seven Lights/Eye & Tooth:

nor *(Creation: Light & Darkness)*

cast *(Division: Firmament)*

your pearls *(Ascension: Sea & Land)*

before the **pigs**, *(Testing: Governors)*

lest they *(Maturity: Swarms)*

trample them *(Conquest: Crystal Sea)*

with their feet, *(Glorification: Gentile Dominion)*

and having turned, *(INCENSE – Transformation)*

they tear you *(MEDIATORS – Vindication: Torn VEIL)*

to pieces. *(SHEKINAH – Representation: Scattering, Dominion)*

THE CHARACTER

Now to the identity of these dogs and pigs. How are they similar? Dogs and pigs are scavengers. They "eat death." The instances of "worms" (maggots) in the Bible have the same meaning, whether they are eating over-ripe manna or the flesh of King Herod.

At this point, Jesus' sermon is all about judgment. A righteous judge is not a hypocrite. But then Jesus speaks about dealing with unrighteous judges. Being scavengers, dogs and pigs are not discriminating despite the fact that they have heard the Law:

> For it would have been better for them never to have known the way of righteousness than after knowing it to turn back from the holy commandment delivered to them. What the true proverb says has happened to them: "The dog returns to its own vomit, and the sow, after washing herself, returns to wallow in the mire." (2 Peter 21:22)

These dogs and pigs are judges whose law is the flesh, whose god is their belly. But why does Jesus employ images of two animals? How do such dogs and pigs differ from each other? The answer is that they minister in different domains.

THE ARENA

Dogs scavenge within the house, or within the city (1 Kings 14:11; 1 Kings 21:24; Psalm 59:6). Pigs are the scavengers *outside* the walls, eating not household scraps but agricultural refuse, as they do in the parable of the prodigal son.

A similar combination of dogs and pigs is found in Isaiah 66, where Israel's holy sacrifices are deemed unholy. For her profane sacrifices, Israel is ready to be "deconsecrated." Once again, the references to the offerings correspond to the architecture of the Tabernacle. The dog is linked to the table, and the pig is linked to the husks of the threshing field.

These lines are the "Ethics" section of the stanza:

> Offering an ox = slaughter of a man
> *(Bronze Altar, Land)*
> Sacrificing a lamb = breaking a dog's neck
> *(Golden Table, Firstfruits)*
>
> Offering grain = offering pig's blood
> *(Lampstand, Pentecost/Harvest)*
>
> Offering incense = blessing an idol
> *(Incense Altar, Trumpets)*

The animal offered at Firstfruits was a lamb (not a choice between a lamb or a kid as it was at Passover). Dogs and lambs meet again in Matthew 7:15: "Beware of false prophets, who come to you in sheep's clothing but inwardly are ravenous wolves." Dogs have to do with the source of doctrine, the priestly house.

> [Jesus] answered, "I was sent only to the lost sheep of the house of Israel." But she came and knelt before him, saying, "Lord, help me." And he answered, "It is not right to take the children's bread and throw it to the dogs." She said, "Yes, Lord, yet even the dogs eat the crumbs that fall from their masters' table." Then Jesus answered her, "O woman, great is your faith! Be it done for you as you desire." And her daughter was healed instantly. (Matthew 15:24-28)

The Jews would not allow any holy flesh or oblations to be given to dogs, only the unclean meat which they themselves were forbidden to eat (Exodus 22:31). Jesus uses dogs to highlight the mistreatment of the common people by the Jewish rulers. Again, dogs are linked to the Table, the "Firstfruits" Man, the blameless Jew:

> There was a rich man who was clothed in purple and fine linen and who feasted sumptuously every day. And at his gate was laid a poor man named Lazarus, covered with sores, who desired to be fed with what fell from the rich man's table. Moreover, even the dogs came and licked his sores. (Luke 16:19-21)

Paul likens the post-Pentecost Circumcision to dogs in God's house:

> Look out for the dogs, look out for the evildoers, look out for those who mutilate the flesh.
> (Philippians 3:2)

Pigs possess a cloven hoof, like the clean animals, but were unclean because they do not chew the cud. Symbolically, this has to do with a failure of judgment. Rumination is an image of meditation. Pigs lack kingly wisdom.

> Like a gold ring in a pig's snout is a beautiful woman without discretion. (Proverbs 11:22)

It seems that dogs are false priests in the house (Garden) under a pretense of serving God, much like the sons of Eli, or the false prophets in the time of the kings. The pigs are indiscriminate rulers of the Land, hence the reference to them "walking on the pearls of wisdom" (the "Sea" being a reference to the king's court, as the Laver symbolizes the crystal sea, the court of heaven). Dogs and pigs are the Church and the State "on the take."

THE END

Based upon these definitions, dogs and pigs are priestly and kingly scavengers who cannot discern the truth because they walk in the flesh.

At the Last Supper, Judas was a dog sent from the house. Jesus deliberately gave him "that which is holy," His own sacrificial body, and Judas returned with the pigs—to attack and scatter the disciples.

In reference to Jezebel, it is worth mentioning that the "Covenantal" parts of her were too unclean for even the dogs to eat: her head (Garden: priest), hands (Land: king) and feet (World: prophet).

Finally, who are the pigs in the next chapter, Matthew 8? Some believe their significance is linked to a Roman garrison situated nearby. It is more likely they were a sign to the Jewish rulers, the kings of the Land (1 Kings 10:23; Revelation 6:15). The demoniacs were victims of an unfaithful priesthood, scapegoats for a government which refused to judge righteously. The demons would be cast into those who ruled over them, who thought they dwelt in the courts of God, but could

Jehu's Companions Finding the Remains of Jezebel
Picture from The Holy Scriptures, Old and New Testaments,
Stuttgart, 1885. Drawings by Gustave Dore

not "walk on the sea." The reversal would be the same as it was between the rich man and Lazarus, which identifies the context of that parable.

We see one final, but very subtle, link between the dogs and the pigs, the rulers of the Garden and the Land, a corrupted Church and State, in Revelation 17:18:

> And the woman that you saw [Jerusalem as Jezebel: dogs] is the great city that has dominion over the kings of the Land [the Herods as Ahab: pigs].

There are no dogs in the New Jerusalem, because her King is the Lamb:

> Outside are the dogs and sorcerers and the sexually immoral and murderers and idolaters, and everyone who loves and practices falsehood. (Revelation 22:15)

SILVER IS BRIDAL, BUT THE SILVER BRIDE IS UNITED IN HER GOLDEN TONGUE.

13

A TONGUE OF GOLD

THE TYPOLOGICAL SIGNIFICANCE OF THE SIN OF ACHAN

"...every tongue should confess
that Jesus Christ is Lord..."
(Philippians 2:11)

Philippians 2:5-11 retraces the biblical Covenant pattern. If we align the pericope with the flow of the history of the establishment of Israel, the logic in the author's arrangement and choice of words becomes more apparent. We shall look at the structure of the passage and then discuss the significance of the literary placement of the famous phrase "every tongue."

SWEET COUNSEL

Let this mind be in you which was also in Christ
Jesus, who, being in the form of God, did not
consider it robbery to be equal with God,

> but made Himself of no reputation,
> taking the form of a bondservant,
> and coming in the likeness of men.

> > And being found in appearance as a man,
> > He humbled Himself and became obedient
> > to the point of death,
> > even the death of the cross.

> > > Therefore God also has highly exalted
> > > Him and given Him the name which is
> > > above every name, that at the name of
> > > Jesus every knee should bow,

> > of those in heaven,
> > and of those on earth,
> > and of those under the earth,

> and that every tongue should confess that Jesus
> Christ is Lord,

to the glory of God the Father.

(Philippians 2:5-11)

TRANSCENDENCE

Day 1 – Mind of God/Robbery from God
(Genesis - Sabbath)

HIERARCHY

Day 2 – Bondservant
(Exodus - Passover)

ETHICS

Day 3 – Obedience to death
(Leviticus - Firstfruits)

Day 4 – Exaltation
(Numbers - Pentecost)

Day 5 – Investiture
(Deuteronomy - Trumpets)

OATH/SANCTIONS

Day 6 – Every tongue
(Joshua - Atonement)

SUCCESSION

Day 7 – The Father's Glory
(Judges – Booths)

The cycle begins with the Son's rest in the Father (Sabbath), and His delegation to be our Passover. Leviticus concerns the ascension offering, the Firstfruits Man. Numbers is a book of *Testing* in the wilderness, the rule of heaven upon the earth, with Israel as stars, ruling lights, in the darkness. When Israel failed to rule over sin, the nation was threshed and cut off. In the wilderness, Christ refused to bow the knee to the devil (Matthew 4:8-9), so now every knee will bow to Christ.

Then, the words at Day 5 allude to Exodus 20:4:

> You shall not make for yourself a carved image, or any likeness of anything that is in heaven above, or that is in the earth beneath, or that is in the water under the earth.

These are the three levels of the cosmic Temple, miniatures of which were the ark of Noah and the Tabernacle of Moses. What was the context of Exodus 20:4? Recreations of the Creation in precious metals as false gateways to God, false mediators. Jesus was not only the true Temple, but as glorified Priest-King He now reigned over the angels, the Jews and the Gentiles.[1]

angels, (Heaven) - Most Holy Place
Jews (Land) - Holy Place
and Gentiles (Sea) - Temple Courts

[1] This pattern is established in the worshipers at Jesus' birth: first the angels, then the Jewish shepherds and the Gentile wise men.

As "Day 5," the apostolic witness summoned a New Israel, an assembly with Sanctuary access and thus Gospel authority over all three of these domains. Thus, the Revelation not only shows us the retirement of the angels and their replacement by a human government in heaven, but also the dissolution of the Jew-Gentile divide, the end of the Temple's mediatory sacrifices.

There was plenty of bronze, silver and gold in the Tabernacle and Temple, but mediation for the nation was by flesh and blood: the animals and the Man of Day 6. Day 6 concerns the Covenant Oath.

THE BRIDAL RESPONSE

This is where the "tongue" comes in, and the Bible Matrix enables us to align and systematically verify correspondences that are otherwise invisible. At Step 6, *Conquest*, Atonement (coverings), we have the High Priest and the Covenant Oath, the Lord requesting a "confession" from "Adam," as Mediator between heaven and earth, that the nations might be blessed. In the Babel narrative, God scatters the tongues and the "lip" (religious confession[2]) of the nations before they can be united at Step 6.[3] In the sixth book of the Bible, we read of Achan's theft of a "tongue" of gold, along with 200 shekels of silver and a Babylonian robe (Joshua 7:21, 24), from Jericho, a city "devoted" to God

2   See *Bible Matrix II: The Covenant Key*, 208-209.
3   See *Bible Matrix*, 83.

as Firstfruits of the Land. In the Revelation, the "loud voice" consistently appears at line 6 in many stanzas. And in the structure of the entire prophecy, Jesus comes with His bride at *Conquest* with a sword in His mouth. Just as the Oath promises obedience, so the Confession of the people defers to the obedience of the Mediator. Every week in our worship, God requires a "unity of tongue" in Christ before we can ascend into His presence to worship as representatives of the nations.

> Likewise deacons must be reverent,
> not double-tongued... (1 Timothy 3:8 [NKJV])

Just as there was an empowering "unity of lip" scattered at Babel, the "gate of God," which meant that nothing they proposed would be impossible for them (Genesis 11:6), so there was no double-mindedness in Christ, the High Priest who became the torn Veil. He possessed "integrity of tongue," that is, no satanic guile. He sent His Spirit who enabled a unity of confession in the Firstfruits Church so that nothing could be withheld from her (John 17). It was impossible for the elect, Greater Eve, to be deceived by the promises of the false prophets of post-Pentecostal Judaism. Silver is bridal, but the silver bride is united in her golden tongue.

TONGUE AND ROBE

A golden tongue is a symbol of a pure confession. For the saint, this is the answer of a good conscience towards God (1 Peter 3:21). Gold signified the holiest

Achan's Sin
from *The Story of the Bible* by Charles Foster
Drawings by F.B. Schell and others (1873 - 1884)

features of the Tabernacle. Gold is pliable and heavy ("glorious"), pure and eternal. It cannot corrode, so its nature remains consistent.

Holiness is thus an integrity of confession, a unity of deed and word, a correspondence between the testimony of the mouth and the witness of the life. Tongue and robe are head and body, Word and Government.

Achan's tongue of gold and Babylonian robe were symbols of a false integrity, a "Babelic" unity manufactured without reference to God—the kingdoms of the world for the price of the knee bowed to Satan, a repeat of the sin in Eden.

Adam's sword was his tongue. Instead of testifying to God's Law when it was challenged, Adam listened to the "golden tongue" of the "shining one," an angel of light, the false Lampstand in the Garden. Adam stole from God. He hid this false tongue of gold and the promise of a robe of a false unity, a false kingdom, from the eyes of God. He failed to possess the Land. We never hear another word from Adam.

> If I speak in the tongues of men and of angels, but have not love, I am a noisy gong or a clanging cymbal. (1 Corinthians 13:1)

Israel also failed to possess the Land. Her condemnation began at the first Pentecost, where she took the Covenant oath and was punished for her misuse of the gold of Egypt. Three thousand perished after drinking the powdered gold of the idol, the image of a beast.

Achan's sin threatened the Covenant Oath taken by a new generation of Israelites and their possession of the promised inheritance. The tongue and robe were false *Word* and stolen *Government*, with the rebellious Man unwilling to be the obedient *Sacrament*.

TONGUE LASHING

The Lord's intention in every case is that the Word from heaven might purify the Mediator (or priesthood), and that this Mediator/priesthood might then speak this Word to purify the nations.

WORD: angels, (Heaven) - Most Holy Place
SACRAMENT: Jews (Land) - Holy Place
GOVERNMENT: Gentiles (Sea) - Temple Courts

At the center of the Bible Matrix (Step 4), the fiery tongue of the Law executes the Sanctions upon Israel and purifies her, as we see in the book of Numbers.

At Step 6, it is the fiery tongues of the newly-purified, newly robed (baptized) members of Israel executing the Sanctions upon the nations, as we see in the book of Joshua. As with all prophets, all mediators, Israel gets tongue-lashed in the wilderness, then Israel becomes the tongue-lasher in the Land.[4]

This explains the apparent contradiction between

---

4 See *Bible Matrix II: The Covenant Key*, 195, for a diagram which demonstrates how the fivefold Torah relates to the sevenfold Dominion pattern.

the judicial stoning of Achan, his family and his livestock, and Deuteronomy 24:16, which prohibited the execution of Israel's children for the sins of their fathers. Achan's punishment was an echo of the ban upon the first city of Canaan rather than the Covenant Sanctions upon Israel. He was not "tongue-lashed" as an Israelite but as a Gentile. He had not coveted his neighbor's house and contents (Exodus 20:17), but that which belonged to God (Joshua 22:20).[5]

He was condemned as a Canaanite, but also as part of Jericho, the "Firstfruits" of the Land, a whole burnt (ascension) offering in which "all flesh" was cut off.

ADAM

WORD: God (Father)

SACRAMENT: Man images God (Son)

GOVERNMENT: Animals submit to Man (Spirit)

ACHAN

WORD: Achan as his own "captain"

SACRAMENT: Achan's offspring in the Land

GOVERNMENT: Achan's livestock as wild beasts

Through unbelief, Achan put his entire house outside of Israel and under the ban. Through faith, Rahab saved everyone in her house, an event which resembled Israel's

---

5   In the Ten Words, the commands against theft and false witness (the sins of Achan) are followed by the two commands against coveting (house and contents), which together align with the Feast of Booths (ministry to the Gentiles), and the Covenant Succession of Israel. See *Bible Matrix II: The Covenant Key*, 63.

Passover. The house of Achan bore the judgment of the house of Rahab, and was buried under a pile of stones.

These two houses represented two brothers, Perez and Zerah, the sons which Tamar bore to Judah. Rahab married into the Messianic line of Perez, and the cutting off of Achan's family ended the line of Zerah.[6]

UNCLEAN LIPS

The fiery words of the prophets threatened Israel with the fate of Jericho. Coals of fire from the Bronze Altar were used to set "devoted" cities alight during holy war.

In Isaiah 6, the "raw" prophet is a man of unclean lips, the "Firstfruits" of an Israel who has not kept her vow. By the Spirit, he becomes a human "fiery one," a *seraph* sent to wage holy war on a nation who honored God only with her lips (Isaiah 29:13; Matthew 15:8). The king failed to repent and Jerusalem was burned.

Likewise, Revelation is the story of the apostolic holy war against an Israel united against—and *blaspheming*—the Spirit of Christ. The final biblical instance of the three level "tongue-lashing" process was the threshing of Judah with the testimony of Jesus in the first century. Revelation pictures the apostolic witness as fire, smoke and sulfur coming from the mouths of holy war horses (9:17), the aroma of life to some and of death to others (2 Corinthians 2:16). The fiery tongues

---

6   This reversal resembles the twofold "blessing and cursing" of Jericho and Israel in chapter 10 of this book, and also the reversal of the fates of Naaman and Gehazi mentioned in chapter 14.

of Pentecost were the warning of a greater fire to come: Word, Sacrament (martyrdom), Government. The war horses of the nations are summoned by the fiery chariots of the prophets.

In rebellion against the Word, the Herods manufactured their own Pentecost, calling down their own "fire from heaven" like the priests of Baal on Mount Carmel (Revelation 13:13). This revolt began with the proclamation of the king's speech as the voice of a god and not a man (not an *Adam*, Acts 12:22-23), a sacrificial beast with the horns of a lamb but the mouth of a dragon, who set about devouring the saints.

This rejection of Christ's authority culminated in the completion and celebration of Herod's gilded Temple in AD64. Spiritually, this was an "image of the beast" crafted by a corrupted Aaronic priesthood while Christ, as a better Moses, was away on the mountain. It was a dumb idol which "came out of the fire" and miraculously spoke with a golden tongue.

In their loyalty to the Herods, the Jewish rulers became the old "Numbers" Israel, cast out in the wilderness as children of Egypt. However, the Judaizers within the Church were members of the new Israel who, like Achan, had smuggled in items which were devoted to destruction, the "elementary things" of a worship centralized on earth (2 Peter 3:10).[7]

---

7   This is presumably why Paul refers to the Judaizers in Galatia as "troublers," a reference to the Valley of Achor. See *The Shape of Galatians: A Covenant-Literary Analysis*, 21-23.

So that Jesus (Joshua) might inherit all nations, both the golden tongue of the Herodian priesthood and the Babylonian robe of their Roman statism were cut off. Again, Jerusalem was burned with fire.

A HEAVENLY TONGUE

A tongue of gold is Covenantal language. It is either the pure Word of God from the Sanctuary, or the gods of the nations set up in the Sanctuary. It is the Law of God in the mouths of men and women refined by the fire of the Spirit, or it is a demonic lie on the lips of an idol which cannot speak. How does this apply today?

The ministry of the Church post-AD70 is to conquer the World in the same way in which the apostles conquered the Land, uniting all nations in a single "Covenantal" confession of faith. How can we carry this out when the Church herself is so divided?

The execution of the Sanctions upon Israel divided those who kept the vow, the Covenant Oath, from those who did not. This process could only bring death, a constant division, a whittling of Israel down to the family of Achan.

The New Covenant, however, has better promises. Our salvation rests in the fact that Jesus kept the Covenant Oath on our behalf (His mission in Philippians 2:5-11), and thus we can go and do likewise—in the power of the Spirit.

Pentecostal (international) unity is Jesus' "tongue of gold," a spring which can bring forth only blessing upon the elect of God (James 3:12; Numbers 22:18). Blessed by the fiery tongue of Him who took our curse, we are now to bless all nations with the Gospel, taking their curses as a witness to them. We need no Babelic tongue of gold because we *are* tongues of gold, the confessions of a good conscience towards God.

> But Balaam answered and said to the servants of Balak, "Though Balak were to give me his house full of silver and gold, I could not go beyond the command of the Lord my God to do less or more." (Numbers 22:18)

NAME ABOVE ALL NAMES

With this background we can understand the placement and meaning of "every tongue" in the literary structure of Philippians 2:5-11. It refers to a global testimony concerning Jesus Christ, the Man who is Himself the New Covenant. The words of His Father at His baptism and transfiguration will be echoed by every member of every nation. In the end, through the witness of the saints, no one will be able to deny the faithfulness of Jesus Christ the righteous. Every tongue, and every language, will confess that He is Lord. But what of the Babylonian robe?

The motivation of the Babel builders was the making of "a name for ourselves" (Genesis 11:4). Since the Father has given Christ a name above every name, the conflict is now between unity in His name and unity in ours. History since AD70 has been a long succession of attempts, both religious and secular, to unite the nations without true obedience to Christ. But there can be no true or lasting kingdom (Government) that is not inherently priestly, that is, Sacramental. The attraction of the robe of Babylon will finally give way to the seamless robe of Christ.

A WORLD OF INIQUITY

The context of Jesus' words is always Covenantal:

> The one who rejects me and does not receive my words has a judge; the word that I have spoken will judge him on the last day. (John 12:48)[8]

So is the context of James' warning about the tongue:

> So also the tongue is a small member, yet it boasts of great things. How great a forest is set ablaze by such a small fire! ... From the same mouth come blessing and cursing. (James 3:1-12)

Achan betrayed Israel's renewed Oath and "second" circumcision, and his stolen tongue became a curse. A bridled tongue is a circumcised tongue, a bound sacrifice. We mortify our tongues from cursing that they might only bless. With holy tongues faithful to our own Joshua, we are to set the world on fire to avoid the flames of judgment.

---

8   See *Bible Matrix II: The Covenant Key,* chapter 15, "The Liberating Curse."

THE BLINDNESS
WHICH CAME
UPON ISRAEL
ACCORDING TO
THE FLESH
AFTER PENTECOST
WAS A "SCALY"
LEPROUS MIND.

14
SCALES OF JUSTICE

THE COVENANTAL SIGNIFICANCE AND SERPENTINE NATURE OF BIBLICAL "LEPROSY"

"They shall take up serpents..." (Matthew 16:18)

The linguistic root of the word translated "leprosy" [*tsara'ath*] may mean "smiting." The curse of leprosy came as a "stroke," which aligns it with the plagues the Lord brought upon Egypt at the hand of Moses. This, however, gives us no clue as to what this disease actually was.

The "whiteness" of this condition most certainly links it to the "whiteness" of death. The purification rites for a person contaminated by a corpse are similar to those for a person with "leprosy." Moreover, when Miriam is struck with the condition, Aaron begs that she not become like a still born child "whose flesh is half eaten away." However, there is another feature of this "leprosy" which traces this "death" back to Eden.

Whereas the Hebrew word denotes being struck with a plague, it is described in Akkadian with a word which means "scaly" or "covered with dust." Scales and dust tie it to the curse upon the serpent in Genesis 3. Leviticus 13 also refers to a "dry scall," so rather than naming an actual disease it describes a symptom: scaled skin.[1]

This might help explain the language connected to it in 2 Kings 5, where the leprosy of the faithful, obedient Gentile is transferred to the lying, thieving Israelite, as his ironic Covenant "inheritance":

> The leprosy therefore of Naaman shall cleave unto thee, and *unto thy seed* for ever. And he went out from his presence a leper as white as snow. (2 Kings 5:27 [KJV])

Naaman comes from the Hebrew verb *naem*, which means "pleasant, beautiful," with the idea of "gracious" or "well formed." (As with some other biblical characters, it may not actually be the real name of the person described in the narrative.) It seems that Naaman is the "bridal man" in this story, as Jacob and David and Solomon in earlier history. But his whiteness is the

---

1 Jacob Milgrom translates the biblical "leprosy" as "scale disease" in his *Leviticus 1-16*, 768–889. In his *Interpretation of Dreams in the Ancient Near East*, Oppenheim quotes the word which has been translated leprosy as "covered with dust" or "scaly." The Akkadian word "epqu", which was translated leprosy in the Chicago Assyrian Dictionary, also means "scaly."

whiteness of a curse, a *de*-formity. A scaly one smitten, a "cleaving," and "seed for ever" are reminders of Genesis 2 and 3. For his covetousness, Gehazi's lineage would image the seed of the serpent.

The whiteness of "leprosy," I believe, pictures priestly linen and burial clothes. It is a spreading "leaven of death" that affected people, clothes and houses. If the link between these possibly very different problems is a dusty or scaly appearance, then the Levitical directions concerning physical blights are clearly seen as "trainer wheels" for ethical ones.

It is fascinating that a smitten Israelite, once he became completely white, could be pronounced holy by the inspecting priest. This was a sign that justice had been entirely satisfied.[2]

Since whiteness denotes a "bridal" purity in the people of God, why is it associated with a curse upon the skin?

When Jesus' robe became "shining" at His transfiguration, He became like the teacher in the Garden of Eden, the serpent, the "shining one." He had kept the Law and was qualified for His final battle.[3] Presumably Adam would also have received a white robe had he defeated the serpent. This forfeited robe was symbolically the glorious skin of the serpent, a token given to him as a mantle of victory. Just as the Pharaohs of

2 The same goes for the whiteness of bones, which I believe were also "holy," though they still communicated uncleanness. See *God's Kitchen: Theology You Can Eat & Drink*, chapter 25, "Bone and Flesh."
3 See chapter 8, "Internal Law."

Egypt wore a cobra crown as a "third eye" of wisdom, so the Man who out-crafted the wisest beast wore its now white pelt as a memorial, a public testimony to its death.

The defeat of the serpent required the completion of the Triune Office, priest, king and prophet, in a single man. Adam did listen to God with a priestly ear, but he failed to rule over sin as a faithful king, and failed to testify against the serpent as a true prophet.

PRIEST *(Firstfruits)*: Priestly bread and priestly robes were white. Manna, the bread intended to humble Israel, was white.

KING *(Pentecost)*: The thrones of Solomon, the wisest earthly king, and of Christ, the wisest heavenly king, are also white, the colour of "eye and tooth."[4]

PROPHET *(Trumpets)*: If Adam had been a faithful prophet, he would have received the fruit of the Land and the fruit of the womb unhampered by the curse. The color of "seed" is also white, and as the fruit of righteousness Christ is holy seed, holy flesh and holy skin.

THE TRIUNE MAN *(Day of Coverings)*: The High Priest wore linen on the Day of Atonement, but removed it after the blood was sprinkled in the Most Holy Place. This pictured the death of Christ. Shedding the cursed skin of the serpent, the linen burial clothes were left in the ground, in the dust.

---

4   See *God's Kitchen: Theology You Can Eat & Drink,* chapter 24, "Horns of Moses."

So, is a white robe a symbol of life or death? Whiteness, true or false, has to do with "legal witness" under the Covenant Oath. The first mention of leprosy in the Bible is in Exodus 4. If "leprosy" described a scaly skin, this would unite for us the two "witnesses," the miraculous signs, given to Moses for the court of Pharaoh, the serpent king. If these two signs failed, Moses was to perform a third, which anticipated the pollution of Egypt's river of life (Exodus 4:1-9):

PRIEST: GARDEN
Rod > Serpent > Rod
(Serpentine **Tree**: Adam)

KING: LAND
Hand > Scaly Hand > Hand
(Serpentine **Flesh**: Cain)

PROPHET: WORLD
Bowl of River Water > Land > Blood
(Serpentine **Offspring**: Noah)

In the New Testament, Herod's Jerusalem has grown into another Egypt. The cross of Christ is the serpentine tree, the self-exaltation of the Jewish rulers is the serpentine flesh (the seed of their father, the devil). The false doctrine of the Judaizers was a flood intended to carry away the Church (Revelation 12:15), but it led to the shedding of innocent blood, the martyrdom of the apostles. The "days of Noah" flood came suddenly in the form of Gentile armies (Daniel 9:26).

SWEET COUNSEL

The preaching of the apostles resulted in the "bowls" of Covenant wrath being poured out upon the Land, which included the first Mosaic curse:

> Then the third angel poured out his bowl on the rivers and springs of water, and they became blood. (Revelation 16:12)

SCALED EYES

The *Physical* Levitical curses pictured *Social* and *Ethical* curses. The curse "May you be stricken with leprosy and blindness" is of very ancient origin, which might explain why Paul had scales fall from his eyes—a sort of "circumcision" of the serpent. After all, this is what the Gospel is doing now: cutting off the evil one by opening the eyes of those who hear it. Like Adam, Paul's eyes were opened to the truth.

Pentecost moved the "scale" from Physical to Ethical, from flesh to sight. The blindness which came upon Israel according to the flesh was the uncleanness of the dust, a "scaly" leprous mind. The ceremonial whiteness of Israel's rites became the whiteness of Gehazi, the sepulchre, and Lot's wife—a memorial to a cutting off. It was a skin that should have been shed and left in the grave.

The Conversion of Saint Paul (c. 1600-1)
Caravaggio

SERPENTINE WISDOM WAS NOT A DANGER TO SOLOMON BUT A ROD IN HIS HAND AND FIRE ON HIS TONGUE.

15
SNAKES AND CHAINS

"When Paul had gathered a bundle of sticks and
put them on the fire, a viper came out because
of the heat and fastened on his hand."
(Acts 28:3)

The Bible's symbolic language links some odd
things together. Only the visual thinker will
notice that these often disparate objects are similar in
appearance, motion or purpose.

Take, for instance, the visual and ethical correspondence between rods and swords, swords and arms,
arms and snakes, and snakes and chains. Rods,
swords, arms, serpents and chains are instruments of
judgment. It seems they all represent the *seraphim*.

Think visually, here, because correspondence through
motion is important. A *seraph* is a "fiery one." Serpents
are known for their flicking tongues, and flames are
known to "lick." Perhaps *seraphim*, serpents and fire
are related because all angels are ministering spirits, a

Aaron's Rod Changed to a Serpent.
Illustration from the 1890 Holman Bible

"flame of fire." They move like lightning. They enlighten and they animate. Evil angels darken minds (with false light), paralyze through oppression and animate for evil purposes through possession. In every case, however, the spirit is but a minister of a word. Angels, serpents and fire are God's tools for *Testing*. Whether good or evil, they are extensions of authority. They are not sons. They are merely servants.

Now, angels are fire, and fire is serpentine. But serpents are also rods. Rods are extensions of arms, for the expression of dominion (used in both travel and government) and for the purpose of discipline. Thus, angels, serpents and rods are all instruments of instruction and discipline. Angels administered the Old Covenant as our teachers. They were rods in God's hand, an extension of His Fatherly authority. The "shining one" in the Garden was a minister of God, despite his worst intentions. And he still is. His deception has always resulted in greater purity and wisdom for the Church. This was exactly the strategy of Solomon in discerning the hearts of the two prostitutes. Serpentine wisdom was not a danger to Solomon but a rod in his hand and a fire on his tongue.

Rod and tongue together are a flaming sword, a *seraph* flanked by *cherubim* at the Sanctuary of God. Rod and tongue are linked in holy war. A *seraph* carried a coal from the heavenly altar to purify the lips of Isaiah. A coal from the altar signified God's intention to cut off a city and burn it as a devoted offering.

Isaiah's words against Israel would purify the four-cornered Land as an extension of the altar. Under the ministry of the fiery prophets, it was now Israel who was under the ban. Yet the kings saw these prophets as traitors, as snakes.

It was the Lord's own hand which touched the mouth of Jeremiah. He put his words into Jeremiah's mouth. Jeremiah, however, became more than a rod. He was a rod with certain modifications.

> You are My battle-ax and weapons of war:
> For with you I will break the nation in pieces;
> With you I will destroy kingdoms...
> (Jeremiah 51:20)

Faithful rule results in growing dominion. In travel (horizontal dominion), a rod connects hand and foot. The Man has crushed the serpent, taken possession of its wisdom, and is enabled to move beyond the Sanctuary as a representative of God Only Wise.

Jesus told Nicodemus that the serpent on the pole was an image of the cross. The cross divides time into past and future, humanity into believer and unbeliever. It is a tool of both death and life. When Jesus took up His cross, the serpent became a minister of Man.

> The cross is only death until you grab it by the tail. Then you will rule by it. It will be a throne. You will do signs by it. It will be a word to the world. Then by the cross, you will divide from sin, and divide from death, and be divided off as one of the holy. Then

they may believe that the Lord, the God of our fathers, the God of Abraham, the God of Isaac, and the God of Jacob, has appeared to us.[1]

When Jesus was lifted up as a bronze (fiery) serpent on a pole, He was a fiery Word of Wisdom on the pure lips of a Man of War, and a wooden rod in the hand of God. He was obedient as a fiery *servant*, not glorified as a Son. As in Exodus, serpent devoured serpent.

The Lord is a man of war; The Lord is His name. (Exodus 15:3)

Peter denied "the Name" at a fire of coals. Jesus restored Peter at a coal fire. Both were altars, Bronze and Golden.[2] Peter's new mission was just like that of Jesus. After His resurrection, Jesus was preparing Peter for holy war, commissioning His disciple as a human *seraph*. The death of the martyrs was a weapon in His hand, and Satan would soon be crushed under their feet.

At the Ascension, Jesus *became* the Father's right hand. At Pentecost, the Church became the rod of Christ in that hand, receiving holy lips, the testimony of Jesus. The apostles' words and deaths—wise as serpents, harmless as doves—were a holy war against Jerusalem. The great city would be sacrificed, just as Jericho was. There would be blood and fire and smoke.

---

1 My friend Luke Welch, commenting on Exodus 4:1-6; 17.
2 For more on the architecture of this event, see "Breakfast At Dawn" in *God's Kitchen: Theology You Can Eat & Drink*, 301.

SWEET COUNSEL

At Pentecost, Spirit-animated men with tongues of fire marched out to take dominion with their sword-words, ministering life and death in the Land. These apostolic witnesses had the heads of lions and tails like serpents (Revelation 9:17-19).

A tongue sets the world on fire, and Jesus, through the apostles, fought fire with fire. The Herodian dragon desired to devour the fledgling Church with the "strange fire" of false doctrine, but it was the Spirit-filled Church which devoured Jerusalem. With wisdom from a better Adam, the Woman devoured the dragon. The final victory arrived when Jesus came to rule with His *mouth,* His *hand* and His *foot.*

> From his *mouth* comes a sharp sword with which to strike down the nations, and he will rule them with a *rod* of iron. He will *tread* the winepress of the fury of the wrath of God the Almighty. (Revelation 19:15)

In Revelation 1, the Church pastors were seven stars, a new Lampstand, a light to the world. But this rod is symbolized in various ways depending upon motion and purpose. In Revelation 20, the unified saints were not a rod but a great starry chain which bound the strong one who had previously held them captive. The Church, as a chain, became a fiery serpentine rod. This was poetic justice for the bondage which Satan, the first heavenly serpent, had administered in Eden.[3]

---

3   For more on the sacrificial process of binding Satan,
    see *God's Kitchen: Theology You Can Eat & Drink,* 125.

SECULARISM

JESUS' DEATH
MADE MARTYRDOM
THE PRUNING OF
A FRUITFUL TREE.

16

ARMED WITH DEATH

MURDER VERSUS MORTIFICATION

"Whoever sheds the blood of man,
by man shall his blood be shed,
for God made man in his own image."
(Genesis 9:6)

When the issue of capital punishment is raised, the Church rightly looks first to the New Testament, then to the Old, but rarely gets as far back as Genesis.

The themes of the early chapters of Genesis are brief and tightly bundled, and all subsequent Scripture unpacks them in greater and greater ways. Because spineless modern theologians are unwilling to stand for the complete veracity of the Bible's foundational book, and yet very willing to jettison basic logic, they often miss the significance of its early chapters for the rest of the Bible and of history.

159

To answer the question of the righteousness of capital punishment from the Bible, one must first ask what a human is, what death is, and what a sword is. The problem for most Christians who take their theological lead from Western culture rather than from God is that the humans, the death and the sword in Genesis 3 are not historical events at all. They are merely ideological symbols.

Christians without a truly biblical worldview are unable to answer these questions. If one believes Genesis is history, then one believes not only that the killing of inconvenient unborn infants and old people is wrong, but that the killing of animals for food and of murderers to atone for their crimes is right.

THE SANCTIMONY OF HELL

Of course, when secularists hear that anyone believes that capital punishment is a crucial part of successful government, there is the unleashing of the sanctimony of hell. "How can you reconcile such a view with your Christian beliefs?"

It amazes me how secularists see their moral code as a development, indeed, an enlightened improvement, upon the tenets of Christianity. This is the result of years of evil in universities and legislative bodies. For our youth, it is the curse of intellectual blindness. Decades of doing what is right in our own eyes has brought us to the point where good is considered evil and evil is considered good. Behind the self-righteous veneer of eloquent speeches, we subsidize sin at home and abroad with public money, promote sexual anarchy and label those who point out its consequences as bigots and haters, we ridicule or demonize our best and most faithful citizens and adore the "victims" of their bigotry, and we pander to murderers while we hack the unborn to pieces. Worse, we enforce this demonic "moral code" through manipulation and deceit, historical revisionism, unjust laws, fraud, intimidation and intergenerational theft. Like Elijah under the rule of Ahab, anyone who dissents is seen as a trouble maker (1 Kings 18:17).

AUTHORITY TO KILL

James Jordan's contribution to the study of any particular book of the Bible is invaluable, but perhaps the most important is his work on Genesis. He observes that Noah was the first man to be given the authority to kill another man. Moderns see this as an isolated fact (well, an isolated *mythical* fact), but it is a fact that is part of a process. The *Testing* of Adam was designed to bring him to a level of judicial maturity. He was given the Law not merely that he might not be a lawbreaker, but that he might *become* the Law, and execute lawbreakers. Who was the lawbreaker? The serpent, who intended to use the Law to bring about the deaths of Adam and his wife. As Jesus said, "He was a murderer from the beginning" (John 8:44).

Adam was to judge the serpent, perhaps to crush its

161

head. He would have brought death into the world through his faith and righteousness, rather than through his faithless unrighteousness. This judgment and death were part of God's plan. Adam was to judge between ethical light and ethical darkness, and mortify sin in his own members and those of his household by dismembering the serpent. (The Lord did "dismember" the serpent in a limited way, just as the curses upon Adam served as limitations.)

So, instead of going boldly from the Garden with flaming sword in hand as God's representative, Adam was cast out of the Garden, and kept out by the sword. He was *under* the sword in chapter 2 but intended to be *over* the sword in chapter 3 as a minister of God, with the heavenly government of the angels upon his shoulders. We see the same thing in Israel, where the new nation is *under* the angelic sword at Passover, but wielding the angelic sword *upon* Jericho. This process of judicial maturity for Israel was intended to lead to a state comprised of self-governing people, an entire nation of judges, of *elohim*. Instead of Israel as the countless stars promised to Abraham, we have the book of Judges, with only its twelve.

The murder of Abel by Cain led to the "ministry of murder" of Lamech, and then a world filled with violence. This is often assumed to be anarchy but it was a kingdom without mercy, a barbarism-by-law. The same satanic manipulation of the law as a weapon against the weak was evident in the Pharisees and

Herods, and is alive and well today. The curse of death was always intended to be transferred from the hand of the angels to the hands of men, but faithful, merciful men—men like Noah, the first judge, the first true "image of God."

All saints have been under the sword in Christ. Our hearts are circumcised, and we have been slain and resurrected *ethically* in Him. We are to judge rightly in all our dealings because we will one day judge angels, as Adam was supposed to, and as our better Adam did. In the Church, it is excommunication ministered with mercy, that serpents might be crushed. In the State, it is execution administered with wisdom, justice tempered with mercy, that serpents might not gain members and become "upright" dragons.

A FRUITFUL TREE

We also mortify the sin in our members that God might mortify sin in the hearts of others. The Word of God in our mouths is a sword that brings life to some and death to others. But there is another death in the hand of every saint, one that we fail to identify as a weapon, and that is *our own martyrdom,* the witness of Abel. This too is a sword to be wielded. It is a greater weapon than the sword of man because it calls down the vengeance of God.

As the canker devours Western culture, we are called to take a stand. The call to participate in sin has been joined by the censoring of any speech against it. The

John Rogers, the first victim (4 February 1555)
of the Marian persecutions in England.
The banner says "Lord receive my spirit."
John Foxe's *Book of Martyrs*, 1563

saints, however, have a weapon that the opposition does not even suspect, and that is the willingness to make obedience to God "a hill to die on." Communism was a threat when its true believers were willing to die for their cause. This is not the case with secular issues such as abortion and same sex marriage. The persecution of our society's best citizens has already begun but the fight will not be long. Our opponents are not willing to die for their cause. They hide behind twisted legislation, as did the Pharisees and all their seed throughout Church history.

The curse of death is ours to use as a weapon, just as Jesus did. When a dragon dismembers the Church, the Church multiplies its members. Jesus' death made martyrdom the pruning of a fruitful tree. This is Satan's worst nightmare.

> As for you, you meant evil against me, but God meant it for good, to bring it about that many people should be kept alive, as they are today. (Genesis 50:20)

The willingness of saints to suffer and die always brings the sword of the *cherubim* down upon God's enemies to divide them, and then the fire of the *seraphim* down upon them to consume them. It is the ministry of the angels at the gate. As the body of Christ, with the testimony of the apostles, this "sacrifice" is now achieved through the government of heavenly men upon earth: *cherubim* (knife) and *seraphim* (fire) in the hand of the *elohim*.

SWEET COUNSEL

Creation: Day 1/Genesis
God has taken his place in the divine council;
in the midst of the gods [*elohim*] he holds judgment:

> *Division: Day 2/Exodus*
> "How long will you judge unjustly
> and show partiality to the wicked? Selah

>> *Ascension: Day 3/Leviticus*
>> Give justice to the weak and the fatherless;
>> maintain the right of the afflicted and the
>> destitute. Rescue the weak and the needy;
>> deliver them from the hand of the wicked."

>>> *Testing: Day 4/Numbers*
>>> They have neither knowledge nor
>>> understanding, they walk about in darkness;
>>> all the foundations of the Land are shaken.

>> *Maturity: Day 5/Deuteronomy*
>> I said, "You are gods [*elohim*],
>> sons of the Most High, all of you;

> *Conquest: Day 6/Joshua*
> nevertheless, like men [*Adams*] you shall die,
> and fall like any prince."

Glorification: Day 7/Judges
Arise, O God, judge the Land;
for you shall inherit all the nations!

(Psalm 82)

DESPITE THEIR
REJECTION
OF THE BIBLE,
MODERN MEN
HAVE FASHIONED
THE GOLDEN CALF.

17
NO COMMON GROUND

BACK TO EGYPT IN SHIPS

"Woe to those who call evil good and good evil,
who put darkness for light and light for darkness,
who put bitter for sweet and sweet for bitter!"
(Isaiah 5:20)

Pope Francis declared in a homily in May 2013 that all people, not just Roman Catholics, are redeemed through Jesus, even atheists.

> The Lord has redeemed all of us, all of us, with the Blood of Christ: all of us, not just Catholics. Everyone! "Father, the atheists?" Even the atheists. Everyone! And this Blood makes us children of God of the first class! We are created children in the likeness of God and the Blood of Christ has redeemed us all! And we all have a duty to do good. And this commandment for everyone to do good, I think, is a beautiful path towards peace. If we, each doing our own part, if we

do good to others, if we meet there, doing good, and we go slowly, gently, little by little, we will make that culture of encounter: we need that so much. We must meet one another doing good. "But I don't believe, Father, I am an atheist!" But do good: we will meet one another there.

This "surprising" exhortation was not in fact a radical departure from Roman Catholic teaching, which identifies good works as Man's *means* of approaching God, rather than as a (non-meritorious) *expression* of our faith in God. This errant definition of "redemption" puts the cart before the horse, but it explains how a commitment to "good works" might be common ground between Catholics and well-meaning atheists.

While there are certainly temporal benefits in the exhortation to do good, both personally and socially, the quickening drift of Western culture away from biblical law is making it increasingly difficult for theists and atheists to *agree* on what is actually good.

NEW COMMANDMENTS

All men are not "redeemed," but all men are indeed *bound* by the New Covenant. They have an *obligation* to Jesus as king. Any rebellion against Him can thus only ever be Covenant-shaped, a counterfeit of the real thing. The "new morality" of Western atheism is not only a rejection of Moses, but also a *replacement* of Moses.

Man cannot live without laws, so to justify his actions, man must *rewrite* the laws. Despite their rejection of the Bible, modern men have fashioned what amounts to a golden calf, a god which will provide all the blessings to which we have become accustomed under God, but without reference to God. Enlightened by biblical law, the finger of modern man has engraved an "evil twin" on the hearts of his children, a moral code which is an exact copy of the Law of Moses, but in relief.

Fumbling around in the darkness of their corrupted minds, they have written their own commandments. Like the Ten Words given to Moses, these laws work from above (Genesis 1) to beside (Genesis 2) to below (Genesis 3), from the source of authority, to the individual, to the nation (corporate). Each in its turn usurps the authority of God over a particular domain, and since the architecture of the original is cumulative, what was intended to be a spring flowing from the Sanctuary as rivers of blessing into the nations becomes instead a source of cursing, barrenness and judgment. Modernism is an idol installed in heaven above, and its idolatry flows down into the Land, and then into the Sea (Exodus 20:4).

ABOVE

Modern man redefined himself through historical revisionism. By rewriting the story of his origins, he recreated himself as the master of his own destiny.

This new story is simply the paganism of *Enuma Elish* given respectability under a guise of science. As in this ancient story, the chaos, unrestrained sex and inescapable death described in the Bible as the result of sin against the Creator are instead enshrined *as* the creator. The curses were reclassified as blessings.[1]

Being the marvelous pinnacle of a world produced by chaos (above), sex (beside) and death (below), Man can be the law *maker* rather than the law *keeper*, issuing decrees concerning chaos, sex and death, able to bless or curse based upon his own arbitrary laws.

BESIDE

However perverse their actions, men must always justify themselves. When an entire culture conspires against God, the justice system becomes the means of this justification. This was the strategy of the Jewish rulers. These men were not anarchists, yet the New Testament condemns them as "lawless." They replaced the laws of God with the laws of men, and unlike God, they were not merciful when their laws were broken.

Likewise, it is not modern Christians who are the Pharisees now. The cult of *respectability* (the nominal Christianity against which A. W. Tozer battled) has become the cult of *immorality*. The godless actually preach immorality as morality, and are more sanctimonious about it than any moralist you could ever meet.

When a Christian points out sin based on God's Law, he is "doing evil," because such lawlessness has

---

1   There is no chaos in Genesis 1. Shapeless and empty, the earth was nonetheless orderly, although requiring forming and filling. Chaos did not come into the world until after Adam sinned.

THE TEN COMMANDMENTS OF THE SECULAR STATE

TRANSCENDENCE

1. Statism. *(One god)*

2. Democratism. *(Allegiance to Man's own voice/name)*

HIERARCHY

3. Environmentalism. Secularism.
   (Permanent fallow/No Sabbath)

4. Easy divorce. Same sex marriage.
   (No mother and father. No inheritance.)

ETHICS

5. Abortion (infanticide) and euthanasia. No capital
   punishment. *(Murder)*

6. Confused and predatory sexuality coupled with
   encouragement of such behavior through
   government support and propaganda. *(Adultery)*

SANCTIONS

7. Taxation, wealth redistribution, and
   "Quantitative Easing." *(Theft)*

8. Historical revisionism (including Naturalism).
   "Progressive" judges. Media bias. *(False Witness)*

SUCCESSION

9. Government corporatism and militarism.
   (Coveting the house)

10. Government control through welfare and public
    education. *(Coveting those in the house)*

The Presence of the Lord Appeared as a Fire on the Top of the Mountain
(illustration from a Bible card published in 1907
by the Providence Lithograph Company)

become enshrined as a rival moral code.

Those who reject what the new Man deems "good" must be cursed. Those who reject what he deems "evil" will be blessed. This is why the witness of the saints is so often legal testimony in the courts of men.

BELOW

Rebellion *above* and *beside* has forced moderns to fashion a false church to fill the holes left by the true one. Since there is no Father in heaven, there can be no fathers on earth, and the state becomes a *goddess*, not only a surrogate mother but a harlot, a single parent struggling to keep order over a household of delinquents. Leaving behind the "childishness" of religion has resulted in a culture of entrenched immaturity.

BEYOND

Modern Western culture is being divided by the testimony of Jesus. Unwittingly, those who reject Him have dug for themselves a Jesus shaped grave, to be cursed under the Law of Moses. That which they fashioned to save them from the conviction of the Spirit has also inoculated them against His grace.

The idol they have placed "above" in their story of origins has finally corrupted every domain. What Pope Francis has failed to realize is that the atheist's "good" is not God's good. He is calling for us to meet with atheists on common ground, but that ground is fast disappearing.

175

NOBODY EXCEPT
CHRISTIANS WANTS
TO TALK ABOUT
"SUSTAINABLE
SEXUALITY."

18
GOD GAVE THEM UP

MODERNISM'S TALKING BEAST

> *"Now therefore fear the Lord*
> *and serve him*
> *in sincerity*
> *and in faithfulness.*
> *Put away the gods*
> *that your fathers served*
> *beyond the River and in Egypt,*
> *and serve the Lord."*
> (Joshua 24:14)

From Sinai to Jordan is a ten day journey, yet, after sinning against the Lord ten times like Pharaoh did, the Israelites wandered in the wilderness for forty years like Moses did. The pattern of events between Egypt and Canaan sheds a great deal of light upon the sexual confusion in Western culture today, and God's remedy for it.

40 YEARS OF HARLOTRY

Priests and people both offered "strange fire," expressed firstly in spiritual and then physical adultery. The chaff was threshed, the dross consumed, in the holy fire of the Law of Moses, the Covenant Ethics.

This process of "threshing" appears at the center of the Bible Matrix. In the festal calendar, it corresponds to the time of the wheat harvest, which is why Pentecost was the time of the giving of the *Law* from heaven, and the sending of the fiery *Spirit* from heaven. In the Creation Week and Tabernacle, it is the seven burning eyes of the Lampstand, the government of heaven (sun, moon and five visible planets) watching over Israel. In the Covenant pattern it is the "Ethics," the section where God lays out the rules for success. In the rite of sacrifice, it is the holy fire.

Related to threshing, the process of grinding the grain to flour with a millstone is a biblical euphemism for sexual relations, whether faithful or unfaithful. This corresponds to the other symbols because under the Lawful eyes of God, Israel is either shown to be a faithful bride or an adulteress. Is the fire of her desire true or "strange" (that is, foreign)? This exact pattern serves as the underlying structure of James 1:15, a sentence in which the apostle presents sin as a process which twists every single one of the symbols above. It is a sick parody of Creation and Covenant because it begins with entertaining darkness as light, a false word from a false god. Like obedience, disobedience results in an abundance, but in plagues instead of plunder. And instead of achieving success and longevity, both personal and corporate, it brings death.

TRANSCENDENCE

But each one is tempted
(Day 1 / Ark / Sabbath)

HIERARCHY

when he is drawn away
(Day 2 / Veil / Passover)

ETHICS

by his own desires
and enticed
(Day 3 / Altar & Table / Firstfruits)

Then, when desire has conceived,
it gives birth to sin;
(Day 4 / Lampstand / Pentecost)

and sin, when it is full-grown,
(Day 5 / Incense / Trumpets)

OATH/SANCTIONS

brings forth death.
(Day 6 / Mediators / Atonement)

SUCCESSION

(No Future)
(Day 7 / Godlikeness / Booths)

(James 1:15)

The only reason a new Israel came out of the wilderness is because God made a "new Covenant." He had already prefigured this to their fathers through the giving of a second set of tablets to the nation after the sin with the golden calf. Between the first set and the second, the worshipers were executed under the testimony of two witnesses, the original tablets of Moses. The second set was, for all intents and purposes, a "new" Sinaitic Covenant.

ETHICS

○ *Ascension:* The First Tablets

◎ *Testing:* The Golden Calf & Judgment

◕ *Maturity:* The Second Tablets

Likewise, at a greater level, there was the initial (dual) giving of the Law at Sinai, and a second giving of the Law, hence the name *Deuteronomy,* which means "second law." Between these two Covenants, the entire old generation was buried in the wilderness. She was consumed by God's jealousy, as demonstrated to her on Sinai and in the destruction of the golden calf.

ETHICS

○ *Ascension:* The Tablets given by God

◎ *Testing:* Old Israel dies in the wilderness

◕ *Maturity:* The Law repeated by Moses

Moses Breaks the Tables of the Law (Exodus 32:19)
Gustav Doré, Doré's English Bible (1866)

So, the pattern found in the initial giving of the Law was a microcosm of the entire journey, with *Numbers* as the fiery "Pentecost" of the greater pattern. Old Israel thus became the golden calf incarnate, Egyptian idolatry carried as a household god in the hearts of fearful men and women.

The man-made attributes and fictitious origins of the golden calf were by no means arbitrary or accidental. But what do they mean? To understand the faithless culture which now surrounds us, we must understand what this idol represented.

TRANSCENDENCE: Its miraculous origin was a silly lie. It is the nature of an idolatrous culture to profess to be wise and progressive even as it becomes increasingly gullible and backward (Romans 1:22).

HIERARCHY: Having received the instructions for the Tabernacle, Israel knew that God Himself regarded gold as a symbol of the holiest things. Gold speaks of kingly authority in heaven. However, it is the Bronze Altar which corresponds to the ox or calf. The ox is not a *kingly* symbol but the leader of the priestly *servants*. The blood of a bull was offered for the priesthood on the Day of Atonement. The Bronze Altar was bronze, not gold, because it spoke of the *priestly submission* of earth to the king of heaven. And in Solomon's Temple, the oxen which carried the Bronze Sea were themselves fashioned out of bronze. As a servant, this altar was located outside the tent, not inside as a son or an elder. The ox was natural, not supernatural, and a slave, not a son. Thus, the golden calf was itself a symbol of a rebellion of God's "firstborn son," who wished to return to the slavery of Egypt's king and his gods.

ETHICS: This golden ox "came out of the fire" at the first Pentecost. Holy fire falls upon the servant-ox, offered in place of human rulers. The ox does not come out of the fire, at least not as an ox. It must be transformed into a "swarm," a new "heavenly" body, bridal smoke that is pleasing to God. A golden ox coming from the fire announces that natural things are acceptable to God, that no transformation is necessary, that an earthly ox in this fallen world is every bit as holy as the beasts which surround the throne in heaven. This is the same deception as that of the dragon in Eden, who promised to the first priest a kingdom which avoided the refinement of holy obedience.

OATH/SANCTIONS: It is faithfulness under the fire of testing which brings an abundance, plunder instead of plagues. Here, Israel had taken the plunder of Egypt and fashioned it into a plague, just as the Philistines later did after the Ark of the Covenant felled their false god and struck their cities.

The golden calf was still considered by Israel to be plunder, which is why the judgment of God concerning it was perfectly just. It was ground into powder, that is, a "swarm," a plague, and its worshipers drank it as a jealous inspection concerning the Covenant Oath which they had made. The harlot who consumed the cup would herself be consumed.

SWEET COUNSEL

TRANSCENDENCE

Moses delays on the mountain, and the people desire that Aaron make a god. *(Creation - Sabbath)*

HIERARCHY

Aaron gathers the plunder of Egypt and "engraves" it into a calf, replacing the "graven words." *(Division - Passover)*

ETHICS

Aaron builds an altar and proclaims a feast (a table) *(Ascension - Firstfruits)*

God sends Moses down and desires to consume them with fire. *(Testing - Pentecost)*

Moses hears them singing, and grinds the calf into a powder, a "swarm." *(Maturity - Trumpets)*

OATH/SANCTIONS

The people are divided between the blessed and the cursed. The idolaters die under the sword of the Levites. *(Conquest - Atonement)*

SUCCESSION

Moses offers himself in place of Israel for the sake of her future. *(Glorification - Booths)*

Pictorially-speaking, Israel drank the golden calf as if it were a swarm of consuming locusts. Liturgically, the "insides" of the idolaters were exposed, just like the adulteress in Numbers 5, before they were consumed externally, by the "flaming sword" of the priests.

SUCCESSION: But, as God revealed to Moses, this episode was not finished yet.

> "But now go, lead the people to the place about which I have spoken to you; behold, my angel shall go before you. Nevertheless, in the day when I visit, I will visit their sin upon them." (Exodus 32:34)

The remainder of Israel died over the next forty years, but out of the furnace came a new Israel. This national or "corporate" forty years was the fruit of a previous *personal* one, the time Moses spent in the wilderness. This also was a period of fiery "threshing."

40 YEARS OF FAITHFULNESS

Moses spent forty years in the wilderness. He saw the "Lampstand" of God in the holy place on the mountain. Like Israel after him, he too came out of the wilderness with uncircumcised children to conquer a city. His exile began with his rejection by Israel as their judge. The righteous sentence he passed and executed upon a single Egyptian (as an Egyptian prince), he would now carry out upon the entire nation of Egypt with the power of God. This forty years matured Moses, and it also matured Israel. Their previous rejection of him had sentenced them to another generation of slavery, but now he, they, and Egypt, were all ripe for a harvest. But before even the preparation of Moses, there was a greater time of growth.

Over a period of 400 years, Israel grew to fruition

from a tribal family to a nation. As the other bookend to the nation's history, Israel's "times of the Gentiles," from Malachi to Matthew, was a similar period of 400 years spent waiting for a deliverer. Both periods were silent as far as words from God. He was waiting until the seed had come to fruition, until the words spoken by the prophets had done their work.

As with Moses, the 400 years was followed by a period of 40 years. Jesus, as a better Moses, covered the personal wilderness wandering in the 40 days of His temptation, reflected in Moses' time on the mountain.

However, the "corporate" testing was indeed 40 years, the time between Jesus' ascension and the end of the Old Covenant, from Pentecost (AD30) to Holocaust (AD70). Those forty years, from the tearing of the veil to the destruction of the Temple, allowed both righteousness and sin to become full grown, to bring the hidden things to light. The sacrificial sword of the Gospel, applied by the Spirit of Pentecost, would reveal the thoughts and intents of the hearts of Israel.

So, four hundred years, forty years, and forty days are time spans allowed by God for things to come to fruition: the National (400 years of generations); the Judicial (40 years, one generation); and the Personal (40 days for one man, the Covenant Head). God allows time for the words spoken to men and women to become flesh in every realm, that they might expose their true natures in every realm.

IN THE NAME OF LOVE

It should be no surprise that we can see similar patterns in our culture, which was founded upon and then progressively, deliberately, shaped by the Bible.

It is over 400 years since the Reformation, and the "cultural capital" of this great event is now running dry. We can be confident that this means God is doing something new, and something bigger, but also that there are some "birth pangs" ahead of us.

Although there have been highs and lows since the Reformation, the wholesale hatred of the Bible we are witnessing today would have been unthinkable in any previous era. The seeds for this have been sown in various ways over hundreds of years, but the slandering of the Scriptures and the rejection of biblical morality has taken only one generation. Like ancient Israel at Sinai, we too have "broken loose," but how has this been expressed in modern culture?

It is 40 years since the introduction of easy divorce. It promised freedom but has only brought slavery and death. It promised plunder, but has instead brought plagues. The body count of the sexual revolution in the USA alone, if limited to a consideration of abortion, is over 50 million. But this "redefinition" of marriage that men and women might more easily "break loose," and the "redefinition" of the unborn that they might be disposed of without blood guilt has undermined every other human definition. As it was with the golden calf, this confusion begins with a silly lie concerning origins. Since it is the events in Genesis 1-3 which define humanity, the breakdown of modern society is following a predictable pattern.

Firstly, our children do not understand the difference between *men and women* (Garden – Word), what their roles are when joined as *husband and wife* (Land – Sacrament) or how those roles as *father and mother* shape future society (World – Government). The old "Tabernacle" has been torn apart. Not only does every man do what is right in his own eyes instead of what is right in God's eyes, he will defend it with a sanctimony unparalleled in the Church's history. Just as René Girard opened our eyes to Jesus as the scapegoat, we now see our only source of true *blessing,* the Word of God itself, being *blamed* for many of our problems.

Thankfully, like Jesus, the Bible will rise again, vindicated before its enemies.

With darkened minds, those who are now lobbying for the "redefinition" of marriage ignore the social destruction we have experienced over the past four decades. Relaxing the marriage laws caused untold confusion, suffering, abuse, misery, mental health problems, sexual confusion, disease, and incalculable financial cost to our culture. The very thing that promised freedom led to bondage in every area of life. The best way to sell slavery is to package it as liberty. Of course, this required that individual responsibility and self-government be slandered as slavery.

Today, these deluded people assume that things will just keep ticking along as they now are without any further consequences. Predictably, other distortions are already queuing up for their "freedoms," requiring more boundaries to be broken. And those who approve of same sex marriage will have no valid argument against worse perversions. They will have dismantled those arguments to get what they wanted, just as their cultural "parents" dismantled marriage laws forty years ago. When this happens, their objections to these other distortions will seem just as shrill, small-minded and bigoted as Christian voices do now.

There is a threefold pattern occurring right before our eyes. In Romans 1, Paul speaks of God "giving people up." He uses the phrase three times because "threshing" is a threefold ethical process:

ETHICS

Ascension: Therefore *God gave them up* in the lusts of their hearts to impurity, to the dishonoring of their bodies among themselves... (Romans 1:24)
False Altar – Law Given: External Law

Testing: For this reason *God gave them up* to dishonorable passions... (Romans 1:26)
False Fire – Law Opened: Carnal Pentecost

Maturity: And since they did not see fit to acknowledge God, *God gave them up* to a debased mind to do what ought not to be done. (Romans 1:28)
False Smoke – Law Received: Internal Law

Notice the progression. It is sacrificial, a golden calf "formed" that comes out of the fire "filled" as a plague. This is why Paul describes them as "filled" with all manner of unrighteousness. So, at which point are we now? We are seeing the Strange Fire written into Law. We are surrounded by a dying generation that rebelled knowingly, and a younger generation that has no idea of God's Law. This perverse legislation is a "Deuteronomy," a "second law" invented by the wicked which condemns the next generation to death, not life. Unlike Deuteronomy, it prepares them not for *Conquest* but for defeat; not for prosperity but for disinheritance. That puts Western culture at the beginning of the third step, a body of carnal people united against God in the name of love, a false Church worshiping its own image. Just as the Judaizers were described as locusts in the Revelation, devouring everything in their path, so we have an apostate Christendom in its death throes. It is a sick parody of the Covenant process because it began with a "false word."

At heart, the disease of our culture is not environmental or economic but ethical. The Law was given. The Law was opened. The plagues we are currently experiencing—disease, sexual confusion, hatred of God and His Law—are a "swarm" that will "torment" us "for five months" (locusts swarmed from May until September, from Pentecost till Atonement). The current debates prove that God is not mocked. We all reap what we sow.

Since we are following a biblical pattern, what is on the horizon? There is a sword coming, a sword that will divide those who love God from those who hate Him, divide those who have found a covering for sin in Jesus Christ from those who stand exposed to the consuming fire of His wrath. Our very culture is being torn in two by a Levitical sword. At this point, the divide is becoming apparent not only in politics but in demography. We are quite willing to sacrifice the future of our culture for "sexual freedoms" now. However we spin it, and as little as we might like it, sex is about children, and children are the future. Sex is always tied to the future.

"Sustainability" is a current buzzword, but nobody except Christians wants to talk about "sustainable sexuality." Only marriage has a long-term future, and God will keep following this "Covenantal" pattern of testing, maturity and exposure/covering until all the saints are gathered.

Many dispute these predictions, but a tree is always known by its fruit. As marriage is finally destroyed through "redefinition," another 40 years will see us become even more predatory, lonely, disease-ridden and mentally disturbed, and nearing extinction as a culture—a nation of widows and orphans.

The good thing is that distortions are always short-lived. Call it natural selection. It is not Christians sitting in judgment upon the various distortions of marriage. It is God Himself. History has already vindicated the prophets concerning easy divorce, and history will vindicate those now speaking against this false "resurrection" of marriage in our laws. The results are unavoidable: cultural division and the death of the counterfeit.

What is left for us to do? Continue to gather together, examine our own hearts for the buds of the same plagues that are fully grown in the world, and drink before God the cup which vindicates internal law in us, the work of the Spirit of Christ. And we must keep serving that very cup of testing to the nations through prophetic testimony, no matter much they cry foul, until they stagger and fall, and God raises them up again with contrite hearts and open eyes.

THE LEFT
MIGHT BE
GODLESS,
BUT THE
RIGHT HAS
ONLY THE
FORM OF
GODLINESS.

19
LAMECH'S
PATSY

"I was in prison and you came to me."
(Matthew 25:36)

From the New York Times:

U.S. PRISON POPULATION DWARFS
THAT OF OTHER NATIONS

The United States has less than 5 percent of the world's population. But it has almost a quarter of the world's prisoners.

Indeed, the United States leads the world in producing prisoners, a reflection of a relatively recent and now entirely distinctive American approach to crime and punishment. Americans are locked up for crimes—from writing bad checks to using drugs—that would rarely produce prison sentences in other countries. And in particular they are kept incarcerated far longer than prisoners in other nations.

Criminologists and legal scholars in other indust-
rialized nations say they are mystified and appalled
by the number and length of American prison sentences.[1]

How do we explain this phenomenon in the most
Christian country in the world?

In *Godless: The Church of Liberalism*, Ann Coulter
explains how naïve the Left is for believing that everyone can be rehabilitated. Fair call. She observes that the
reason the prison population has grown is that crime
rates have fallen. If crime is the problem, incarceration
is the solution. Vengeance is the answer.

The cases that Coulter documents do demonstrate
that the Progressives have made some tragic mistakes
concerning convict releases. Regardless of this inepti-
tude, it does appear that they have more of a heart than
their Conservative counterparts. They might not
believe in "sin," but they do believe in mercy.

In a country which is being divided by Christ like the
two goats on the Day of Atonement, or the sheep and
goats in Matthew 25 (generally speaking), the easiest
political solution for the moral majority is to fix the
blame upon a scapegoat.

James B. Jordan has discussed Rene Girard's theory
regarding the communal lust for a scapegoat in various
cultures throughout history. He writes:

> Job as king is the "greatest of the men of the east"
> (Job 1:3). He employed hundreds of people and fed

---

1   By Adam Liptak, *The New York Times*, Wednesday, April 23, 2008.

the poor. The disaster that overcame his household was, thus, a disaster upon the entire realm. The poor were starving, and hundreds of people were either killed or out of work. The sores on Job's body were a sign of the lesions on the body politic of which he was the head, a point no ancient reader would miss...

Job's position as king or leader of his people has been skillfully analyzed by Rene Girard in Job: The Victim of His People, translated by Yvonne Freccero and published by Stanford University Press in 1987. Despite the many flaws in this book, it makes clear that the attack upon Job came not because he was an ordinary person, but because of his preeminent position in this community, which had fallen into chaos seemingly as a result of God's judgment upon Job, their "king."[2]

Once the blame is fixed and the scapegoat, whether innocent or guilty, is punished, things can go back to normal. This is the apparent goal of the accusations against Job. It was definitely the case with Jesus, as predicted by the High Priest. To avert a national crisis, one man would die for the people (John 11:45-53).

SEVENTY TIMES SEVEN

The story of human scapegoating begins with Lamech, the first real king, in Genesis 4. This narrative, like all of Genesis, follows the pattern of the Feasts in the

---

2   James B. Jordan, *Was Job an Edomite King? Part 1,* Biblical Horizons No. 130.

Israelite calendar (Leviticus 23), even though these were instituted many centuries later. Lamech's pronouncement appears at the "Day of Coverings" point in the Cycle. This corresponds to the "Oath/ Sanctions" point of the biblical Covenant pattern, which explains why Lamech's act of judgment, bringing down a curse, is recorded as an oath.

Although Cain built his fortress as the first "city of refuge," his own rejection of the mercy of God, as demonstrated in the rite of substitutionary sacrifice, meant that there was no covering for sin in the culture he founded. Lamech not only fixes the blame, but multiplies it unjustly as capital punishment, upon a young man who struck him. The man was guilty, certainly, but his crime was not worthy of death. In the usurped role of High Priest, instead of turning the other cheek and modeling mercy for his people, Lamech modeled an unrighteous vengeance. Not only are the seven sprinklings of atoning blood (Leviticus 16:14) multiplied into seventy-seven, here it is human blood.

Lamech's speech, as the voice of a god, we might say, is the institution of a legal system without mercy. His personal sin as ruler became a corporate sin. The world was eventually filled with vigilante violence, a society full of "gods." Nobody was willing to cease from their sins, but neither was anyone willing to be wronged and bear it, covering a multitude of sin with love, as the Lord does.

Lamech and his Two Wives (1795)
William Blake

SWEET COUNSEL

We see a similar situation in the first century. Among other things, Jesus called out the Pharisees for their lack of mercy. Note that he was not calling for an end to actual justice, but for the leaders to model the righteous and just, yet merciful, rule of Yahweh.

> Then Peter came up and said to him, "Lord, how often will my brother sin against me, and I forgive him? As many as seven times?" Jesus said to him, "I do not say to you seven times, but seventy times seven." (Matthew 18:21-22)

This gives us a heavenly perspective on the pronouncement of Caiaphas, the High Priest, concerning the need for a human scapegoat. Like Lamech, the Herodian High Priesthood had usurped true atonement, and Jesus was the young man they would slay.

MEDICINE MAN

Perhaps this is the situation in America today.[2] Where the Left fails in the ministry of justice, the Pharisaical Right scapegoats the weak. When good citizens call for mandatory sentences to curb growing crime, they are in fact part of a culture that is attempting to exorcise its own demons. Rich Bledsoe observes that this was most likely the situation with the demoniacs of Gadara:

---

2   Since 2008, some states have reported declining rates of incarceration, but this may be due to less police on the streets. Also, like the "Housing Bubble" and the widely reported "College Bubble," it seems there may also be a "Private Prison Bubble."

A friend of mine who is a Christian clergyman, and is from India, and has demonstrated gifts of exorcism, tells me that the power of the witch doctor is the power of being able to command lesser demons to leave by the power of a greater demon. But the demons are never banished. They just transfer place or position. In the case of this text [Matthew 8:28-34, Mark 5:1-20, Luke 8:26-37], the demons of the village were all put on this one poor man who became a representative demoniac, and bore the pain and agony of the entire community in himself.

There are four descriptors around the demoniac that we need to look at.

Firstly, he is chained, but in his madness is so crazed that he breaks the chains and cannot be restrained. He is the recipient of the accusations of the demons of the village. The very character of the devil is that he is "an accuser" (Revelation 12:10, Zechariah 3:1). Accusation is the most galling of all experiences, and he is accused day and night by the devils who have taken possession of him who used to accuse the community. Now along with the demons, the whole village also accuses him.

Secondly, he is naked. (Luke 8:27, Mark 5:15) This is a symbol of shame, and he thus bears the shame of the entire community.

Thirdly, the text says that he cuts himself with stones (Mark 5:5). In the Greek, the term is *"autolapsis"*, which literally translated means "self stoning." In other words, the madman executes himself by stoning, which in the ancient world was a ritual form of execution. Hence, he is executed on behalf of the community as well. Finally, he lives amongst the tombs, (Mark 5:2, 5) which as a fulfillment of the other curses on him means that he is already dead. He bears death and damnation in himself for the entire the community.[3]

The act of scapegoating is an act of "blame shifting," that is, substitutionary atonement. This means that there is godly blame shifting and ungodly blame shifting. As Bledsoe describes, "shifting" is the work of the witch doctor. In the accounting of sin, it is a form of "cooking the books." The first person to shift blame was Adam (Genesis 3:12), and the second to shift blame was God Himself (Genesis 3:21). God offered a similar "covering" to Cain but was rejected.

Perhaps the desire for a human scapegoat is the inability of fallen Man to take vengeance upon historical Adam, so one man must stand in his place. Of course, the time came when the Man standing in Adam's place was the Lord Himself. This led to unfathomable mercy, but also to the avenging of all the scapegoats in the history of godly witness, beginning with Abel, in the destruction of Herod's Temple and City.

In the end, it is only Jesus, the Great Medicine Man, who can "shift" our sins as far from us as the East is from the West.

---

3   Richard Bledsoe, *The Dysfunctional Family of the Gadarene Madman*, revbledsoe.wordpress.com

COOKING THE BOOKS

With so many in chains, neither more undiscerning "mercy," nor more scapegoating "justice", is the answer. The Left might be godless, but the Right has only the *form* of godliness (2 Timothy 3:5), with no true power. The only real hope is the Gospel, the mercy of Christ, the love of God displayed in His fulfilment of the Day of Atonement on Golgotha. And those of us who are transformed by His forgiveness, with our sins blotted out, are then called to transform others by this same forgiveness, establishing a culture of mercy sourced in the righteousness of God.

A SPIRITUAL
VACUUM
CANNOT
REMAIN SO
FOREVER.

20
THE EXORCISM OF CHRIST

21ST CENTURY ICHABOD

"Rivers of water run down from my eyes,
because men do not keep Your law."
(Psalm 119:136 [NKJV])

The unbelief which constantly confronts Western Christians is a different animal to the demonism found in many other cultures. We do not suffer the full-scale "possessions" seen in paganism. The rebellion is just as self-destructive, crazed and zealous, and just as much a "nothing" as the idols of the pagans, but apparently it is a *different* kind of nothing.

Eastern demonism and Western unbelief are essentially the same thing—nothing, futility, vanity. This means that, once you cut away the lies, the solution is the same—the Gospel. The gods of secularism are the gods of demonism, but the "nothing" is coated in very different lies. This is because one is essentially pre-Christian and the other post-Christian. Unlike paganism, secularism is "high handed" rebellion, a revolt against God which is fully informed about Him.

APOSTASY AS DEFENSE

Old Covenant history was a sequence of "lunges and parries," with God on the defensive for a helpless Israel surrounded by idolatrous pagan cultures. When Israel itself turned to pagan gods, Yahweh disciplined the nation by opening "the doors of the sea" and letting the armies of the nations rush in like a flood (Daniel 9:26).

Under the New Covenant, the roles have been reversed. It is the Gospel of Christ which is on the offensive, flowing out into the nations as living waters. Western apostasy is thus *not* a lunge but a *parry*, not an attack but a defence. Christ is the Spirit seeking to possess, and, despite outward appearances, it is now the nations who are helpless. Secularism is an auto-immune disease. It is an exorcism of the Holy Spirit's life giving work in a constantly invading Gospel. When He is cast out from a culture which knew Him, (in the words of Peter Hitchens regarding the Soviet Union), there is left "a howling void."

Although there is some sense in which a Christian culture without Christ is an entirely new species, it has much in common with first century Judaism, the first godly culture to apostatize and then suffer the onslaught of the Spirit-filling Gospel of Christ.

Head of Jesus (detail)
Gustave Doré

In both cases, the desolate house was built for God but eventually vacated by the Spirit. The first century Ichabod was prefigured in Christ's "giving up the ghost," but began in truth at Pentecost. One generation later, Josephus records that the voices of the Lord's hosts were heard in the Temple announcing, "We are departing hence." The Spirit now dwelt in the Christian Church, which suffered until Constantine gave Western culture a new *cultus,* and consequently a longevity sourced in God. Half a millennium later, the Holy Roman Ichabod began with the martyrdom of the early Reformers. This brought new life to the Church, and eventually a degree of reformation and revival to Holy Rome itself.

Modernism offered a new kind of reformation, one sourced in science and pragmatism, and Christendom expelled the very Spirit which sustained it. Its vacated temple is the institution of the once-Christian state. As with Herod's Temple, the secular edifice contains no images because the temple *itself* is the image.

DEATH OF THE MULTI-CULTI

The multi-cultural experiment began in Christian nations because of their freedom and prosperity. But these gifts were the result of an eternally self-defined and culture-defining Christ. The "undefined" secular square has usurped this role, but the secular square is not self-sustaining.

Published in 2006, Mark Steyn's *America Alone: The*

End Of The World As We Know It, is now slightly dated, but its predictions were astute. Steyn speaks of the "death of the multi-culti." Demographically, the West has exercised its democratic right to extinction:

> The modern western democracy is perfectly feminized in every respect, except its ability to reproduce.

He traces the economic problems of Europe back to demography, low reproduction rates, a loss of the will to survive. The West has become what he refers to as a "soft culture." Its loss of what Friedman calls "self-definition" has made it vulnerable to the "hard" culture of self-defined Islam.[1] The failing demography is the result of a failure of faith. Within a collapsing culture there is an absence of *cultus.* With Christ exorcised, the vacant shell of Christendom is the perfect host. A multi-culture can survive under the *cultus* of Christ, but a *multi-cultus* is impossible in the long term. There must be singular animating principle, or "spirit."

Despite its pretensions, secularism is still only the front porch of a tolerant Christian church. Only Christ can gather all men. Only the Spirit of God can unite the nations. If Christ is exorcised from the culture, the seat of a central, animating *cultus* is left vacant, vulnerable to whichever *cultus* of the cultures allowed in is the most self-defined. A spiritual vacuum cannot remain so forever. Thus the secular square of the West has no

---

1   See Edwin H. Friedman, *A Failure Of Nerve, Leadership in the Age of the Quick Fix.*

defense against the virus of Islam, which is a clever counterfeit of Christianity. Like Christianity, its agents hide in plain sight, their operations are cell-based and decentralized, their cause easily breaches all social and cultural boundaries, and it promotes birth rates far in excess of faithless citizens. Yet, while Islam flourishes under the wings of the West, its own ancient seats of power are disintegrating before our eyes, politically, economically and even demographically.[2] It seems Islam can only survive as a parasite within the disintegrating corpse of the first Christendom.

This is not only good news, it is the outcome of the Spirit of Christ in the Gospel. When God destroys His own Temple, not only is the knockdown for the purpose of building a *bigger* house, He builds that bigger house *out of the invading hordes*.

It is always in the nature of Israel to die for the world, creating in the process a "holy place" in which God can do a greater work. The Church is repeatedly called to get out of its comfort zone and die for the sake of expansion and greater glory.

It is most certainly not the end of the world, but it is the end of the world as we know it, and in a way Mark Steyn cannot even imagine. After Christ is cast into the wilderness, He always returns with greater power to judge the false priests and usurping kings. We live in exciting times.

2   See the statistics in David P. Goldman, *How Civilizations Die (And Why Islam Is Dying Too)*.

HERM
ENEU
TICS

WE MAKE A
SHOW OF THE
AVOIDANCE OF
SWALLOWING
CAMELS IN
ORDER TO
DIVERT
ATTENTION
FROM OUR
PLAGUE OF
GNATS.

21
THE PERILS OF DEEP STRUCTURE

INTEGRITY IN THE DAY OF SMALL THINGS

"My God—it's full of stars!" – David Bowman,
in Arthur C. Clarke's *2001: A Space Odyssey*

The danger inherent in dealing in the "big picture" themes in biblical theology is that it can become self-serving. Observing the generalities can be a means of neglecting the particulars. This is the opposite of the strategy of the Pharisees but it is no less devious. We make a show of the avoidance of swallowing camels in order to divert attention from our plague of gnats.

Just as highlighting the suffering of individuals can be used as a means of throwing big truths into disrepute, so focussing on abstract truths can become a disguise for a failure to deal with sin by actual people.

The heart is deceitfully wicked, able to twist even the best theology into self-serving ideology. True theology maintains a personal, pastoral heart. Speaking against political hypocrisy, Doug Wilson writes:

> One of the temptations that comes to people who learn how to see and identify "deep structures" in a narrative—adeptly twirling chiasms they have found, or anticipatory foreshadowing motifs, or whatnot—is that they sometimes lose their ability to read what is right there on the page. They know that the Mississippi River is a metaphor for life, but don't know that Huck Finn was a boy.[1]

> I agree that the deep structures of Scripture really are there, and that they are both wide and deep. But I also think that hunting for them too readily can prevent some readers from seeing what is right on the surface of the text. Scripture has deep mines— but is also a beautiful landscape.[2]

Is this competition between the basics and the profound universals necessary at all? Are they not complementary? Metanarratives, both true and false, can be used to deceive and oppress. But surely a *true* metanarrative is the "corporate" reflection of truths which must be believed and acted upon in every day life by individuals? Any metanarrative that fails in this regard is not deep structure at all. It might be a mile

---

1   Douglas Wilson, *Doctor, You're Cutting Too Deep. You're Scratching the Table,* www.dougwils.com

2   Douglas Wilson, from the discussion which followed the blog post.

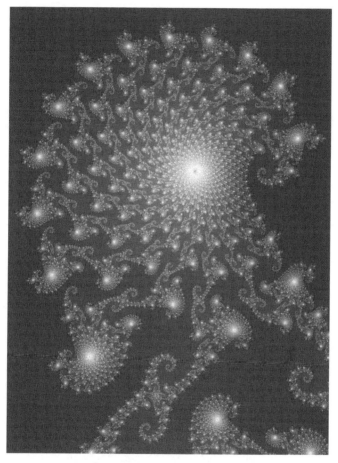

Partial view of the Mandelbrot set. Step 12 of a zoom sequence.

wide but it is only an inch deep. It is a sleight-of-hand which offers a "big picture" utopia without obedience to God in the here and now.

The deep structures of the Bible *do* hammer home the more obvious messages, including practical, personal holiness, just *with a bigger hammer.* This is because the "landscape" itself is anthropomorphic.

The structure of the entire Bible follows a pattern laid down early in Genesis. The Bible begins with Adam, Eve and the serpent and by its end their "personal" sin has multiplied into the full-grown rebellion of institutions: the Man of Sin, the Harlot and the Beast. The corporate oppression of the Pharisees and Herodians was supported by individuals like Saul, who thought the will of God could be achieved by the anger of man (John 16:2, James 1:19-20). But he learned that in Christ's kingdom, the means resembles the end. The Body of Christ is only truly integrated when each individual member is a representation of the Head.

In his commentary on the book of Judges, James Jordan notes the reason why the universal themes of the Bible are represented in the human characters in the book, in real, historical lives:

> There are in Biblical theology certain great universals. They derive from the fact that man is the image, the very symbol of God. Thus, throughout the Bible marches *The Seed.* He is the one born of *The Woman* who will crush the head of *The Serpent.* We shall meet him several times in the book of Judges.

Indeed, the crushing of the head of the enemy is one of the most obvious themes in the book...

But are all these [characters] mere symbols, mere allegorical figures? Not at all. If you or I had written these stories, and had tried to make everything come out just so, we would have had to engage in a little judicious fiction (and there is nothing wrong with that, as Jesus' parables illustrate). But that is not what we have here. These were real flesh and blood people, who really lived. Their lives were so ordered by God, however, that everything did come out just so; and the history of their lives was written by the author in such a way as to bring out the universal meanings, without the need to distort a single fact.[2]

Thus, the Bible itself is both wide and deep, both practical *and* theological. It has complete integrity. There is no need to pit the big picture against the every day because they share the same shape. Failing in the every day makes the big picture impossible, but losing sight of the big picture entails a loss of vision and hope.

Our everyday methods should correspond exactly with our grand narrative. God's tune is the same on the tinwhistle or with full orchestra. At a deep level, for instance, worship is symbolized as commerce[4] (Revelation 3:18; 13:17; 21:24-26), yet the Lord still loves just weights and measures in our business dealings.

3   James B. Jordan, *Judges: A Practical & Theological Commentary*, ix-xi.
4   Holy worship results in the nations bringing their glory to the Sanctuary. See James B. Jordan, *Through New Eyes*, 73.

SWEET COUNSEL

When we dig into God we find more of the same, but with an increasing grandeur. The words on our lips should be the overflow of the depths of our hearts.

Unbelief always takes shortcuts, however well-developed our theological understanding might be. As it was for Adam in the garden, the first step towards inheriting the earth, towards truly biblical horizons, is to be faithful in the day of small things.

MODERN SCHOLARSHIP HAS CONSTRUCTED A "VEIL OF EXPERTISE," A HERMENEUTICAL INDUSTRY WHICH HAS UNWITTINGLY ALIENATED OUR CULTURE FROM THE BIBLE JUST AS THE ROMAN CHURCH DID.

22
TECHNICIANS AND INTUITIONS
ACADEMIA'S LITERARY CRIPPLES

"Deep calls to deep at the roar of your waterfalls;
all your breakers and your waves have gone over me."
(Psalm 42:7)

In Steven Spielberg's 1977 movie *Close Encounters of the Third Kind,* Roy Neary (Richard Dreyfuss) cannot get the image of the Devil's Tower out of his mind. At the dinner table, maddened by this new obsession, he recreates the mountain in mashed potato. Finally, he notices the distress of his family, but he comments, through some tears, "Well I guess you've noticed something's a little strange with Dad. It's OK. I'm still Dad. I can't describe it, what I'm feeling, what I'm thinking. This means something. This is important."

Man was made in God's image, and Man, like God, also makes symbols. The Bible is full of them, and this is because God is an image maker. The level of our understanding of the Bible is directly related to our ability—and willingness—to learn the symbol language of God. Sadly, modern Christians want Jesus, but they don't want His Bible.

What if I told you that the Creation Week, the creation of Adam and Eve, all of the Bible's Covenants, the sacrificial process, all of the speeches of God, all the Tabernacles and Temples, every Bible story, the processes of cooking, of eating, of sex, of gestation, of the work day, of human life, of building a house or founding a nation, all have the same shape? What does this mean? It means that man, the image of God, in all these Covenantal acts, is creating images of God in all these different registers.[1]

We Christians need to become more like Roy, poring over the weird stuff in Leviticus and saying, through tears, "This means something. This is important." We need to learn to see things the way the God Who made us in His image sees them.

Our biggest problem is the constraint of the "sound system" of modern theology itself, which simply does not have the capacity to cope with the "bandwidth" of the Bible. The average theologian, faced with Roy Neary, would look at the Devil's Tower, and at Roy's mound of potato, and see no correspondence whatsoever. "These things are not the same. Look. That's *rock,* and that's *potato.*"

---

1   See the "Covenant-literary" charts at the end of this book.

Devil's Tower, Wyoming by Tim Pearce, Los Gatos

SWEET COUNSEL

How did we get to the point where those who are trained professionals in the study and teaching of the Scriptures have little or no aptitude for it? It certainly explains why they, and now most Christians, think the Bible is so complicated. The whales hear the woofers and the dogs hear the tweeters, but the Sunday morning faithful hear only the tinny radio favorites.

DOWNSAMPLING THE WORD

One problem with modern conservative scholarship is its reluctance to deal with types that are not explicitly described in the text. The typological nature of biblical history is rejected, thus most of its "bandwidth" remains unheard. Because of this "downsampling," the author's intent remains a mystery, the text is not interpreted correctly, and the application is in fact way *off-the-mark*. In many cases, a clumsy "moral" has hijacked the entire passage. Because we are looking for morals, not looking at men made in the image of God, the principles to be drawn from the histories are not incarnate universals prefiguring future redemptive events but abstract principles which can be easily ignored.

Worse, this means that a lot of what is considered *interpretation* is merely *application*. For instance, the failure to read the New Testament as both a recapitulation of Israel in the wilderness (past) leading to the events of AD70 (future) is a prime example. Texts which were intended for the Apostolic Church concerning their legal witness against Jerusalem are applied directly to Christians today. This is why Paul's use of Hagar and Sarah is such a mystery to us.[2] Likewise, Jesus' parables must not only be interpreted with His first audience in mind, but also the looming destruction of their entire world, both the physical and political landscapes. Instead, the prophetic import of His razor-sharp stories, bereft of their fulfillments in history, is watered down to a hazy ideology.[3]

This leads to shallow, generalized preaching which fails to grip the heart. This "abstraction" in teaching and preaching is the bane of the best Bible colleges. They are aware of the problem but blind to the solution. Preaching that is more emotive, or better structured, or "relevant" will only get you so far. What we need is Bible teaching that gets across not just the words of God but the significance of real people in history as *images* of God. Let the Bible do its thing and it will create its own relevance in the hearts of men.

THE FOUR LEVELS

In *Theological Commentary: Evangelical Perspectives* (2011), Don Carson contributed the final chapter, entitled "Theological Interpretation of Scripture: Yes, But..."

Very briefly, his assessment is that the *revival* of biblical theology is a good thing, since it is a God-centered attempt "to transcend the barren exegeses

2   See *The Shape Of Galatians: A Covenant-Literary Analysis*, 155-165.
3   See Joel McDurmon, *Jesus v. Jerusalem: A Commentary on Luke 9:51-20:26, Jesus' Lawsuit Against Israel.*

generated by historical-critical methods," but with the caveat that anything in this revival which is *new* is bad. Thus, no new ground of any consequence has been broken. In his concluding reflections, Carson writes:

> A colleague and friend, Graham Cole, has written a paper developing a model he has used in the class-room. He speaks of four levels of interpreting biblical texts.
>
> At the first level, the Bible itself must be understood exegetically, within its literary and historical contexts, with appropriate attention devoted to literary genre, attempting to unfold authorial intent so far as it is disclosed in the text. At level 2, the text must be understood within the whole of biblical theology, including where it fits into and what it contributes to the unfolding storyline and its theology. At level 3, the theological structures found in the text are brought to bear upon, and understood in concert with, other major theological emphases derived from Scripture. At level 4, all teachings derived (or ostensibly derived) from the biblical text are subjected to and modified by a larger hermeneutical proposal (e.g., Trinitarian action, God's love and freedom, or something vague such as "what was disclosed in Jesus"). Traditional interpreters of Scripture who hold the Bible as the Word of God tend to operate at levels 1 and 2, with the strongest of them making excursions now and then into level 3.[2]

2   R. Michael Allen (Ed.), *Theological Commentary: Evangelical Perspectives*, Carson, 206-207.

I don't know about you, but this to me sounds like a guide to music appreciation by people who have never actually heard music, even in their heads. What sort of person needs to have "4 steps" consciously employed to listen to music? Like music, texts *resonate*. Certainly, we listen, interpret, evaluate, enjoy, but the process is a *natural* one. Our understanding of it increases and becomes intuitive, like surfing. One learns to predict the behaviour of the ever-surprising sea by understanding its depths. Actually *riding* the wave (Level 4?) is hardly an indulgence. *It's the whole point.*

Like music, like the sea, all great literary texts have *movement*. Although there is much helpful material in Carson's chapter, somehow he is unable to see beyond the level of the halting gait of a literary cripple, or the novice pianist practicing her scales. In fact, in one sense, he has the entire process upside down. Level 1 is actually the bottom of the sea.

So far, many if not most supporters of TIS operate at levels 3 and 4. One suspects that one of the reasons why the *Brazos Theological Commentary on the Bible* has, in several of its volumes, proved so unsatisfying is that its writers were operating at levels 3 and 4 while trying to give the impression they were operating at levels 1 and 2. Because readers could not forge the actual connections between text and theology ostensibly derived from a commentary on the text, they balked—and rightly so. For what is really needed is work that shows how levels 1, 2, and 3 should be tied together. One should indulge in level 4 only with the greatest caution, and only after the writer has done a lot of work on the first three levels.[3]

What am I saying? That the first work of the theologian is *not* to deal with the texts at the human level and then work his way out to the fundamental themes. It is the Covenant currents which carry the man, the chords which carry the melody. Neither can be understood in isolation any more than the movements of a surfer can be isolated from the motions of the sea.

God was not made in the image of Man. If we understand the nature of the Creation and the Word, the fundamental themes should be immediately apparent *in the plain sense of the text*. If they are not visible, it is because the symbolic significance of man, and indeed everything in Creation, as conferred upon it throughout the Old Testament, has been overlooked. The vague terms employed by Cole to describe his upper two levels suggest that he speaks of lofty slopes upon which he has never laid foot. But how do I know? Because this is where I live. In a short introduction to biblical structure, I wrote:

> Ancient writers added depth using clever tools like symbols, symmetry, repetition and fractals. Many Bible teachers are not aware of these "shapes," and they try to deal with the strange artifacts remaining in the "flattened landscape" using other means.

3   Carson, 207.

One attempt at compensating for this lack of awareness is the list of rules which Bible scholars have given us for reading the Bible. The list is about as long as the Bible itself and many of the rules *contradict each other.* But the Bible is just like any other well-crafted book. It doesn't need a list of rules because you are expected to dive right in and let the author fill you in as you go along. In the case of the Bible, part of that "filling in" is the repetition of symbols, key words and literary structures.[4]

Even with the limited Hebrew I have studied, I can feel the progression of ideas because they are always presented in the familiar musical rhythm. Each note has a harmony, a typological connection to the big picture. As God deals with a man, so He deals with Mankind.

THE NEW ILLITERATI

Carson's criticism of the disunity in the diverse TIS camp is justified, but he offers no real solution to the problem of the gap between the texts and the theology. Perhaps the real problem is this: On the one hand, we have the conservative thinkers imposing their own one-eyed rules and "assorted grids" onto the text to protect it from abuse, and on the other hand we have the imaginative thinkers very often *ignoring* the Bible's own immanent guidelines.

4   *Reading The Bible In 3D,* 9-10.

Like any book, the Bible is of necessity primarily self-referential, self-alluding. Once it sets the scene, it makes its own rules as it goes along, but it constantly stretches them, breaking new ground, interpreting the old in a new, more mature, more beautiful and intuitive way. And how do we discern the rules? We do it by letting the text move us first.

In a culture where we are constantly besieged with sounds, images and words that speak to us at gut level, it takes a studied detachment to remain unaffected, unravished and unravaged by the Bible's brilliant and relentless sensory bombardment. When it comes to the art of the Scriptures, most of academia is not only numb, it has invented its own unique brand of dumb. We have staffed the conservatoire with the tone deaf. Modern congregations suffer a strange new breed of illiterate, an educated elite deliberately *un*-schooled of native literary instinct.

The study of ancient languages attracts people with certain gifts, but being a linguist does not make one an intuitive reader. Thus, we suffer the various hermeneutical "lenses" proposed by theological interpreters, the limitations and contradictions of which Carson rightly criticizes. It might sound glib, but a truly biblical worldview is not one in which the interpreter provides the appropriate lens: the text itself *is* the lens. Through it, the reader sees the world with God's eyes.

We need less technicians and more intuitions, more instinct. Modern scholarship has constructed a "veil of expertise," a hermeneutical industry which has unwittingly alienated our culture from the Bible just as the Roman Church did. Perhaps the insightful work of James B. Jordan can be summarized in one sentence: He has torn the veil by teaching us to read the Bible as if it were any other good book.

WHAT MADE THE DIFFERENCE BETWEEN THOSE WHO RESISTED JESUS' WORDS AND THOSE WHO RECEIVED THEM? WAS IT INTELLECT? NO, IT WAS GIFT.

23
CURING THE MINDBLIND

HERMENEUTICAL ASPERGERS

"Since we have such a hope, we are very bold, not like Moses, who would put a veil over his face so that the Israelites might not gaze at the outcome of what was being brought to an end. But their minds were hardened. For to this day, when they read the old covenant, that same veil remains unlifted, because only through Christ is it taken away." (2 Corinthians 3:12-14)

It has been said that the measure of biblical truth that we have grasped is not determined by the size of our heads but the breadth of our hearts.

The divide between the head and the heart is an issue of integrity, of holiness. But even within the realm of "head knowledge," the intellectual level of biblical interpretation, there is a sort of left brain/right brain divide. The issue here is not one of holiness. It is one of "intellectual sex."

The brains of men and women are different. It has been said that a man's brain has a box for everything, and that the only rule is that *the boxes never touch*. This is much like systematic theology. Typology, in contrast, is like a woman's brain. Everything is connected, just like the internet. This would be one reason why men do not understand women. Women are making intuitive connections, usually through emotional tags, which men simply do not anticipate or comprehend. This is the reason why theologians with a scientistic bent struggle with biblical theology. Interpretation is not a science but an art. It deals not merely in facts but also in images, in visual tags, in *symbols*.

Men are structure. Women are glory. Systematic theology, the classification of facts, is the essential structure, but the Bible is far more glorious than that. Systematics is a valley of dry bones. Typology *gathers* them, puts flesh *onto* them, and breath *into* them, and they become Greater Eve, an army with banners.

This is a divide that can be traced back to Genesis 1. The heavens and the earth were divided, but they were designed to be married, reunited as something greater than the sum of the parts. The Creation week itself was divided into a process of *forming* and a process of *filling*. Then, within Day 6, Adam was formed and filled, then Adam became the forming authority and Eve the one who would fill the world.

All this means that systematic theology is only half the job. Why do modern theologians have such a problem with fully identifying, let alone finishing, the job they are called to do?

The debate over the theological interpretation of Scripture is due to ignorance of the symbolic nature of the physical world, and this ignorance in turn comes from a failure to interpret the world through the lens of Scripture.[1]

TIN GODS

As with appreciation of art, music and non-inspired literature, reading the Bible involves skills in both forming and filling. Conservative evangelical academia seems to consist mainly of "formers." They cover the necessary basics, the crucial historical and grammatical facets involved in making fundamental sense of a text. But then we need "fillers," those who can join the dots, "read between the lines" with an instinctual literary sensibility based on long term immersion in the imaginative world of the biblical authors.

This is exactly the test faced by Adam. God's single commandment was indeed straightforward, but it left a great deal *unsaid*. Adam was supposed to "read between the lines" based on his relationship as God's son. What was the true intention of the Father? In God's promises, Adam certainly had enough to go on. But the serpent presented himself as the first "expert,"

---

[1] For more discussion, see James B. Jordan, *Symbolism: A Manifesto*, at www.biblicalhorizons.com.

putting a slanderous spin on the text by filling the gaps in the "empirical data" with clever lies.

The same goes for biblical interpretation. Liberal theologians interpret the Bible with a deep suspicion of the Father's intentions. When He forbids certain acts, they pontificate like little tin gods and spew forth a serpentine river of bitter water into the body of Christ. God allows it because it tests and purifies the Church. The spiritual whores suck it up, drink the cup to the dregs, and it exposes them for what they are. But our problem is different. It is not an unwillingness to mature under God expressed in grasping equality with God. It is simply an unwillingness to mature under God expressed in fear of making a mistake.

LESS IS MORE

Adam was the first liberal theologian. However, if Adam had been instead a *conservative* theologian, his success would still have been limited, lacking the judicial initiative which the test was intended to encourage. How so? He would have obediently refused to eat from the Tree of Judicial Knowledge, but *not* figured out what to do with the serpent. "What do you mean I was supposed to crush the serpent's head? You didn't state that explicitly in the text."

The Lord required some intuition from Adam, some anticipation of the Father's intentions for him based upon His earlier promises of dominion. The "ministry of death" required a minister. It would either be Adam or the serpent. The missing information was left out that Adam might have an opportunity to think for himself regarding the execution of the law. If this assertion sounds novel, a consideration of the fact that the entire Bible is written this way might help. We are not only intended to notice the details of the text, but also what is deliberately left out. Robert Alter writes:

> The biblical tale, through the most rigorous economy of means, leads us again and again to ponder complexities of motive and ambiguities of character because these are essential aspects of its vision of man, created by God, enjoying or suffering all the consequences of human freedom.[2]

> Though biblical narrative is often silent where later modes of fiction will choose to be loquacious, it is selectively silent and in a purposeful way: about different personages, or about the same personages at different junctures in the narration, or about different aspects of their thought, feeling, behavior...
>   Since art does not develop in a vacuum, these literary techniques must be associated with the conception of human nature implicit in biblical monotheism: every person is created by an all-seeing God but abandoned to his own unfathomable freedom, made in God's likeness as a matter of cosmogonic principle but almost never as a matter of accomplished ethical fact; and each individual instance of this bundle of paradoxes, encompassing the zenith and

---

2   Robert Alter, *The Art of Biblical Narrative*, 22.

the nadir of the created world, requires a special cunning attentiveness in literary representation. The purposeful selectivity of means, the repeatedly contrastive or comparative technical strategies used in the rendering of biblical characters, are in a sense dictated by the biblical view of man.[3]

TOY SOLDIERS

Conservative theologians are the ones who have kept the faith against the onslaught of liberal theology. They have bravely held the fort like the guardians of heaven. Unfortunately, when it comes to biblical interpretation, they are boring as hell. They are formers, not fillers, and the true glory of the text remains invisible to those under their instruction.

What they do not understand is that we are *expected* to read between the lines to interpret much of the Bible, filling in the blanks not only through faith in God's good character, but also drawing verifiable conclusions with an intuition developed through careful intertextual comparisons.

The reluctance to deal with the meanings of types, symbols, textual structure and sacred architecture which are not explicitly revealed, results in a school of theology which is often clueless concerning much of the mind of God. These courageous Guardians Of The Gallery have little appreciation of the actual art. Like

3   Alter, 114-115.

Adam, they fail to perceive the intentions of God implicit in the text. Such an attitude towards the "letter" can only result in an obtuse obedience, confounding the plan of God concerning Man's growth to ethical maturity. Plain obedience, such as that performed by Aaronic priests, without meditation upon the hidden meanings of the types, can only maintain the *status quo*.

> And when Jesus finished these sayings, the crowds were astonished at his teaching, for he was teaching them as one who had authority, and not as their scribes. (Matthew 7:28-29)

The Jewish scribes also guarded the Words of God but failed to read between the lines. They did not understand that their precious texts were also books of clues. They failed to anticipate that the intention of God was a law greater than the Words of Moses, a glory greater than the kingdom of David, a body where every one of the Lord's people is a prophet. When Jesus came to slay the Law by being slain, to resurrect the Law by being resurrected, to depose the Herods by being enthroned in heaven, even His disciples misunderstood Him.

What made the difference between those who resisted Jesus' words and those who received them? Was it intellect? No, it was *gift*. Those with obedient hearts recognized the voice of the Father in Jesus. The Spirit opened their ears, their minds, and their mouths.

I am not proposing that evangelicalism does not

have the Spirit of God. But it is clear that the Church in general has not moved beyond the basics of the Gospel.

> Therefore let us leave the elementary doctrine of Christ and go on to maturity, not laying again a foundation of repentance from dead works and of faith toward God, and of instruction about washings, the laying on of hands, the resurrection of the dead, and eternal judgment. (Hebrews 6:1-2)

What we are talking about here is a level of interpretation which goes far beyond what is explicitly revealed, and yet is entirely consistent with it.

James Jordan has referred to the Church Fathers as the "Church Babies" because they were at the beginning of the Church's task of making sense of the apostolic texts. We have come a long way, but we still have a long way to go, and further progress is always a gift. It is the opening of the mind by the Spirit of God. Unfortunately, many conservative scholars suffer from a sort of interpretive mind-blindness, a "hermeneutical Asperger's."

THE MINDBLIND

A couple of years ago I discovered I have Asperger's Syndrome. Since such diagnoses only began in the 1990s, many adults like myself are only now finding the reason for the many difficulties which we have struggled to cope with or overcome.

The brains of people with Asperger's are wired

differently. We use a different part of the brain to inter-act with the world. Instead of "going with the flow," we are constantly systematizing, collecting, storing and analyzing data. Although this gives many people with this condition some brilliant gifts, such as easily spotting bugs in computer code, it is socially debilitat-ing. That part of the brain simply cannot keep up with the amount of information, or the number of its sources, required for successful social interactions. Fitting in with "neurotypicals" requires a great deal of impromptu "acting." Though it is no less sincere than normal conversation, there is a certain awkwardness, as though the one with Asperger's "has not been given the script." Responses are often delayed, or even entirely inappropriate.

We can generally cope with one-on-one discussions, especially with somebody we know well, but prolonged interaction, or the simultaneous interactions expected at social events, can be intellectually and emotionally exhausting.

Since there is simply too much data to process "in the moment," much of the analysis takes place *after* the event. "What did he really mean?" "Was he winding me up?" "Did you not realize she was flirting with you?" Or worse, *"Did you think she was flirting!"* We obsess over small details that make no sense on their own but do make sense as part of an unspoken social "language" in which we are not fluent, an intuitive "context" which everyone else seems to be born with but which we must learn "by the numbers." There is always a "veil" which impairs intuitive connection.

Without the ability to interpret body language and other channels of communication, all one has to go on is the spoken word, as though it were written on a page. Personal interaction becomes subject to exactly the kinds of misunderstandings inherent in online text. The faces, the "emoticons" are disabled. Studies have shown that people with Asperger's, whether in conversation or watching people on a screen, focus on the mouth rather than the eye.

This inability to read people is called "mindblindness." Unable to anticipate what the other person is thinking or feeling, or where the conversation is going, interaction becomes awkward, often embarrassing and sometimes even distressing, in many cases leading to anxiety, isolation and depression.

Someone described having Asperger's as feeling like you have been born on the wrong planet. Socializing is something like watching a foreign movie with the subtitles switched off. This is exactly how many moderns—including theologians—feel when reading the Bible.

LITERAL AND LITERARY

The weakness of conservative scholarship, the MindBlindness, the lack of literary intuition, the inability to "read the face" of the inspired text, is the flipside of a crucial strength. But, without discarding the data that has been carefully assembled and systematized, they need to "retrain their brains."

How can we achieve a harmony between hermeneutical forming and filling? How does God do it? By the same means through which He grants us salvation. He transforms the letter of the Law by fire, by the Spirit.

> Now if the ministry of death, carved in letters on stone, came with such glory that the Israelites could not gaze at Moses' face because of its glory, which was being brought to an end, will not the ministry of the Spirit have even more glory? (2 Corinthians 3:7-8)

The Spirit of God is opening the eyes of many to the amazing "bandwidth" of the biblical texts, and through Him we are able to behold Him with unveiled face in greater and greater degrees, until we are indeed "face to face" (1 Corinthians 13:12; 2 Corinthians 3:15-18).

An obvious objection to the "systematic typology" of the Bible Matrix would be: "Is this not just another system?" My answer would be: Yes, but it is an *intuitive* system, which I guess is why some people get it and others do not. It is not a system of classification but a system of *relationships*. The shape, the "face" of the text is recognized that its expression might be read and the author's true intent discerned.

Ironically, having Asperger's, with its gifts of analysis, language, logic, and visual working memory has *enabled* me to read this kind of face. I believe it is the shape of the mind of Christ, an Adam who perceived the Father's goodness, crushed the serpent's head, and on our behalf now sees the face of the Father in heaven (Matthew 18:10). By His Spirit we are able to perceive the connections He has put there for us to discover, able to read His mind and discern both the shape of His plans and the nature of His glory.

BEHIND THE
APPARENT
MADNESS,
THERE IS A
VERY FAMILIAR
METHOD, AND
ONE ACCESSIBLE
TO ALL OF US.

24

MERCURY RISING

THE ART OF INTERPRETATION

"Oh, the depth of the riches and wisdom and knowledge of
God! How unsearchable are his judgments and how
inscrutable his ways!" (Romans 11:33)

Hermeneutics is a big word you learn at Bible
College. It is the study or practice of interpreting
texts in the areas of literature, law and religion.

In literature, discovering the intent of an author can
be an enlightening game. In law, one's life (or life
sentence) can hang in the balance of a judge's interpretation. In religion, besides plumbing the depths of the
mind of God, it is an enlightening game in the balance
of which many lives hang. God has revealed His mind
in His Word, and has also seen fit to give to His people
the often difficult job of interpreting it.

The word "hermeneutics" derives from the story of

the Greek god Hermes (called Mercury by the Romans). Wikipedia says:

> The folk etymology places the origin (Greek: *hermeneutike*) with Hermes, the mythological Greek deity whose role is that of messenger of the gods. Besides mediating between the gods themselves and between the gods and humanity, he leads souls to the underworld upon death. He is the inventor of language and speech, interpreter, a liar, thief and trickster. These multiple roles makes Hermes an ideal representative of Hermeneutics, for, as Socrates notes, words have the power to reveal or conceal, thus promoting the message in an ambiguous way. The Greek view of language as consisting of signs that could lead to truth or falsehood is the very essence of Hermes, who is said to relish the uneasiness of the messaged.

God's Word gives us the milk of the obvious, but it also gives us enough mental steak to boggle the best of minds. One only has to read Ezekiel, Daniel or Revelation to observe that God often speaks in riddles. Proverbs 25:2 says:

> "It is the glory of God to conceal things, but the glory of kings is to search things out."

In other words, God deliberately hides things from us. He is the Father in a game of hide-and-seek who delights in being found, but He will only be found by the faithful. This means that the practice of hermeneu-

"The Mad Hatter's Tea Party," from the Lewis Carroll Story
Alice in Wonderland. Illustration by Sir John Tenniel (1871)

tics never leaves the interpreter unchanged, or even unscathed. Every message from God has a purpose similar to the riddle given by Samson to his enemies. The response allows discernment of the heart.

Whenever the Word of God comes, it is an end to business as usual. He disturbs our stagnant slumber to bring us true rest. Some people taste life, others taste death, and there is conflict between the living and the dead.

God lets His Word loose among us to create new life, thresh out the husks and gather the wheat into His barn. He sends confusion to those who have chosen death and gives miraculous persevering strength to those who have chosen life.

God enrages the unrighteous to multiply their blood-guilt. He calls the sheep out from the goats to bring them home. Eventually, the wicked are cut off, and the redeemed are gathered around the Lord. The Word is a sword that ministers life or death, bondage or freedom; it is living water or a cup of destruction depending upon who is drinking—a "liberating curse."

Even Jesus' parables were a two-edged sword. They forced the believers to wrestle with spiritual truths. They also confused and incited the unbelievers to a showdown that would expose their true natures and hasten their destruction...

Certainly, the Bible is not easy to understand, but this is deliberate. It takes desire, discipline, time, meditation, a childlike imagination—and the indispensable guidance of the Spirit. God sent it not just as spiritual food but also as a regular workout that brings strength and maturity. Like Jacob, we are to wrestle with it, obeying in faith what we have learned before God reveals any more. It is a process designed by God to align us to His way of thinking, to make us wise and mature, able to judge between good and evil.[1]

Astronomer Johannes Kepler is credited with saying that as he studied the universe he was "thinking God's thoughts after him." Like the universe, the Bible is an unfathomably complex work whose complete navigation is impossible. Like the universe, it was designed, through its study, to transform the faithful student. Like the universe, its witness can only be understood by those with a godly comprehension of the difference between the heavens and the earth, and the difference between the image and the reality. Warren Gage writes:

> All theology is poetry. The representation of the transcendent realm of God within the immanent world of man is accomplished by means of metaphor, the most fundamental figure of speech. When the Bible describes God as a Father, or a Good Shepherd, or a Dove, it speaks metaphorically. When we hear about the windows of heaven opening up to pour out the flood of Noah, we must think imaginatively. When Jesus tells us that in His Father's house are many dwelling places, He is prompting us to think logically. But when Scripture speaks of heaven

1   *Bible Matrix II: The Covenant Key,* 171, 302.

as the New Jerusalem, with foundations of jewels and gates of pearl, we are taught to think analogically. Theology and poetry, it seems, are bound up together in the Bible.

Poetry is fundamental to the nature of man as a creature. In the beginning God created man in His image and likeness. It is thus through poetic resemblance that Adam was to understand his relationship to God. He was a creature made in the image of God. He was like God, but He was not God. Poetry requires the ability to distinguish the reality from its image in a proper sense. It is the rational capability to see similarities in difference. It thus requires both logical and analogical capacities. Moreover, it requires not merely mental capacity but also moral imagination. Understood in these terms the first temptation of man by the serpent in the garden was an invitation to believe a false poetry. "You will be like God," claimed the enemy, craftily collapsing the metaphoric distance between the Creator and the creature altogether through a simile not of comparison but of identity. The original sin of man is thus the choice which refuses to distinguish between reality and image. From the very beginning, therefore, we are instructed that a robust poetic imagination is required to understand correctly both the Creator and man's proper place in His creation.[2]

So, there is no such thing as being "morally neutral" when it comes to interpreting the Scriptures. A godless

2   Warren A. Gage, *The Crisis in Protestant Biblical Theology*, 5-6.

heart will inevitably lead to twisted conclusions (2 Peter 3:16). Yet, as Gage laments, there is much disagreement between those who can easily be considered godly and faithful. Once the moral concern is dealt with, does the text of the Bible itself offer any answers to the burning questions which divide us?

Possibly the most helpful—and useful—analogy I have seen is found in Peter Leithart's *Deep Exegesis: The Mystery Of Reading Scripture.* He gives the reader a short object lesson using the movie *Shrek.* Despite the mercurial appearance of the biblical texts, there is an internal logic which becomes apparent to the regular reader who places no extra-biblical constraints upon himself. Behind the apparent madness, there is indeed a very familiar method, and one accessible to all of us:

> My insight, if such it is, into the workings of humor was reinforced and generalized when I watched *Shrek,* a movie that I now tell my students is a goldmine of hermeneutical insight. All the funny parts of that film assume that the viewer has information that the movie does not provide... *Shrek* is impenetrable unless the viewer comes armed with a cache of nursery rhymes, fairy tales, and recollections from popular culture. A viewer ignorant of these resources does not miss some marginal features of the film; he misses the entire meaning. He does not get it.[3]

3 Peter J. Leithart, *Deep Exegesis: The Mystery Of Reading Scripture,* 114-115.

Modern evangelicals simply do not get the "textual jokes" in the Bible. As Bible knowledge decreases, academies are faced with students (and even some lecturers) who might as well be from another culture. The wisdom literature and the prophets were written for people who had memorized the earlier Scriptures, perhaps even by chant, since they were children.

> But as for you, continue in what you have learned and have firmly believed, knowing from whom you learned it and how from childhood you have been acquainted with the sacred writings, which are able to make you wise for salvation through faith in Christ Jesus. (2 Timothy 3:15)

So, when Paul the Apostle takes young Timothy to see *Shrek,* the boy gets it. He not only has all the information required to understand it, he is free to make the connections, unfettered by clueless theological constraints and conventions.

In the apostolic witness, all the riches planted or even buried in the "loamy undergrowth" are drawn upon in a clever, tight, witty and often ironic presentation that not only relies upon a deep familiarity with the source material, but whose events follow a structure laid down in those earlier texts.

This is the apostolic hermeneutic, pure and simple. Matthew can refer to Rachel's weeping for her children as he relates Herod the Great's massacre of the innocents. He can draw on an apparently unrelated text in Isaiah to refer to Mary miraculously conceiving. James can stand up and say "this is that" concerning the Tabernacle of David in Acts 2:16. None of these texts were prophecies of first century events. They are references to the way God does things, and the consistent order in which He does them.

The Book of Revelation is the pinnacle, the finest example of tight, witty, ironic and provocative literary allusion in history. Without a deep grounding in the Law and the Prophets, we don't fully comprehend the voice of the One whom the Father told us has superseded them.

Because moderns approach the prophetic texts as something a little crazy, something from left of field, few commentators even comprehend the actual purpose of these books. Modern commentators ruminate obtusely upon the significance of Princess Fiona's freeze-frame mid-air kick. They treat the Muffin Man rhyme as though it had just fallen from heaven. When they read Isaiah 11, with wide-eyed wonder, they strain over the meaning of the wolf in Shrek's bed, or the quick quip of the smallest of the three bears. They give us a detailed history of the geographical location of Shrek's swamp, as if the gradual accumulation of silt recorded in obscure histories or apocryphal texts is somehow the key to the canonical story. *As if.*

If you as a child were raised reciting (or chanting) the Scriptures as Timothy was, the words and the rhythms would have shaped your thoughts, your dreams, your very imagination. You not only recognized the characters in Paul's teaching, you recognized the *shape* of the stories. Like a little child, you would interrupt Dad's retelling of the story because you already knew what was coming next.

Instead, the Church patiently suffers grave-faced theologians writing long dissertations to present in mind-numbing detail the seven historic views of the mysterious comment of the Magic Mirror concerning Snow White: "Although she lives with seven other men, she's not easy," and, like Snow White, remaining cautiously uncommitted to any of them.

The Bible's built-in hermeneutic is simple. It requires not only faith but also *inculturation* in the Scriptures. So, when Ezekiel or Jesus or Paul or John writes something mystifying, like, "No wonder you're late. Why, this watch is exactly two days slow," much Mercury hath made him mad (Mark 3:21; Acts 26:24).

THE REVELATION
IS IN FACT THE
AUTHENTIC END
OF THE STORY,
A DENOUEMENT
OF THE NATURAL
WORLD.

25
TOMBOYS AND TOTEMS

THE BESTIAL GARDENS OF MEN

"Then they will say to the mountains, 'Fall on us!'
and to the hills, 'Cover us!'" (Luke 23:30)

The following lines by Edgar Allan Poe, slightly reshaped, are the first spoken words in the classic Australian film, Peter Weir's *Picnic At Hanging Rock*:

What we see
and what we seem
are but a dream...
a dream within a dream.

Based on a novel by the enigmatic Joan Lindsay, the film is an experience that clings to you, not merely because it is so carefully and beautifully made, but also because it is a film with secret blades: it is a mystery without a solution, a horror story without savagery, a nightmare in which all the watches stop at noonday.

At The Hanging Rock (1875)
William Ford

On Saturday 14th February 1900, a party of schoolgirls from Appleyard College picnicked at Hanging Rock near Mount Macedon in the state of Victoria. During the afternoon several members of the party disappeared without trace...

The picnic takes place on St Valentine's Day. Although named for a saint, the date is a licence for the expression of natural impulses, the heart of paganism. Along with the use of "pipes of pan" in the film soundtrack, the culture of the schoolgirls is a scrapbook of Victorian fertility symbols. Yet, these passionate obsessions and an awakening sexual desire are strictly bound by the corset of Victorian religion. In one scene, recitation of a personal ode to St Valentine is censored for the sake of the memorization of the curricular *Casabianca*. Like first century Israel, Victoriana is indeed not one but *two* women, the bride and the harlot.

The golden icon is a blessed sylph named Miranda, likened to "the Botticelli angel" by one of her teachers. Both her appearance *and* her disappearance become elements in a sort of sacrificial ascension. Time stops and her potential is suddenly a flower pressed in a vice of tragedy. The end of her childhood is the birth of Venus. Though her purity is gone from the world, the memory of its fragrance fills the imaginations of those left behind, just as the mystery of the missing women corrupts, terrorizes and curses them, one by one.

This dichotomy between nature and nurture is

echoed in the quiet but unsettling tension between conflicting cultures and landscapes. The contrast of the rough Australian stablehand with the young English gentleman is humorous but telling. They do not lock horns but become friends—and possible suspects.

There is real discord, however, between the imported English culture and the dangerous and unforgiving Australian landscape into which its literature, dress and architecture have been confidently transplanted, entirely unadapted. Appleyard College is a manmade Eden, a temple and a greenhouse with boundaries clearly defined, its lush lawns giving way abruptly to brown fields. Moreover, the building in real life, Martindale Hall, was itself a deliberate reconstruction of the English home of the owner's wife for the purpose of luring her to Australia. She never came, and he eventually lost the property in a gambling debt.

Visually, the picnic is also a hopeful transplant. It is a European painting, an English pastoral, carefully recreated in a foreign land. Moreover, the nature versus nurture theme is found even in the disparate "beauty and terror" approaches to the rock itself: the primeval eruptions described ominously by Miss McCraw and the Renaissance esthetic of Mademoiselle de Poitiers are both represented within the party of the missing. Victoria Bladen writes:

> The juxtaposition of rational empiricism and emotive response, evident during the carriage ride, is continued with the girls' proposed ascent of the Rock. For

The Birth of Venus (1486)
Sandro Botticelli

Miranda and Irma it is curiosity; they "wanted a closer view of the Rock" (p.33). By comparison, Marion Quade's reason for wanting to go for a walk is to "make a few measurements at the base of the Rock"; she produces "some squared paper and a ruler" (p.25) yet it is not clear how such measuring would be done. In any event, no measurements are taken and the girls' walk quickly takes on the quality of a mystic pilgrimage. Marion discards her pencil and notebook, "toss[ing] them into the ferns" (p. 38), before they fall asleep at the Rock.

While the natural space is a source of admiration and wonder, it is only superficially and temporarily idyllic, not the nurturing landscape of Virgilian pastoral. The girls become immersed in the landscape to a point where they are no longer in control but become subject to its magnetic, subsuming and devouring forces. The tragedy of *Picnic* is that the pastoral immersion in nature is taken to its extremity; the landscape takes and swallows up the heart of the human group.[1]

Director Peter Weir gives the rock a brooding life of its own. The brutish, volcanic monolith with its totempole profiles, indigenous almost-faces, hangs over the idyllic scene, then tears and devours. Have the women been snatched from paradise and swallowed by an ancient hell? Or have they instead been rescued,

---

[1] Victoria Bladen, "The Rock and the Void: Pastoral and Loss in Joan Lindsay's Picnic at Hanging Rock and Peter Weir's Film Adaptation," in *Colloquy*, Issue 23, Monash University.

released from the unnatural constraints—such as the timekeeping—of high culture by the eternal noon of a timeless land?

Marion: Whatever can those people be doing down there, like a lot of ants? A surprising number of human beings are without purpose. Though it is probable they are performing some function unknown to themselves.

Miranda: Everything begins and ends at exactly the right time and place.

Joan Lindsay's novel was published in 1967. After the story came to her in dreams, she wrote the book in a matter of weeks. She was asked repeatedly if the story were true and repeatedly hedged the question. It seems much of it was based on her own experience in a girls' college.

Lindsay also refused to reveal the solution to the mystery. However, the original manuscript did have an ending, left out on advice from her publisher and not released until 1987. In this final chapter, the reader discovers the fate of the missing women, yet all it does is present a further enigma.

The Aboriginal Dreamtime comes to the fore, with transformations into animal totems, falling rocks and the freezing of time, including, surprisingly, the mathematics and science teacher, Miss McCraw. It is beyond weird.

SWEET COUNSEL

Many lovers of the book reject the final chapter as a fake, or at least as an ugly and unnecessary appendage to the ethereal beauty of this particularly strange and, for many years, "never-ending" story. Yet the reader is indeed given hints of the ending in the earlier chapters.[2]

This analysis is an excuse to recommend today (St Valentine's Day, 2014), a stunning Australian film, but also to illustrate a point about the book of Revelation. The attitude of most Christians towards our own enigmatic "final chapter" resembles that of the headmistress of Appleyard College towards the Rock.

Good morning, girls.

Good morning, Mrs. Appleyard.

Well, young ladies, we are indeed fortunate in the weather for our picnic to Hanging Rock. I have instructed Mademoiselle that as the day is likely to be warm, you may remove your gloves once the drag has passed through Woodend.

You will partake of luncheon at the picnic grounds near the rock. Once again let me remind you that the rock is extremely dangerous, and you are therefore forbidden any tomboy foolishness in the matter of exploration, even on the lower slopes.

---

2 Chapter 3 shows signs of slightly clumsy editing once the contents of Chapter 18 are taken into account. See the commentary by Yvonne Rousseau published along with the missing chapter as *The Secret of Hanging Rock*.

I also wish to remind you, the vicinity is renowned for its venomous snakes and poisonous ants of various species. It is, however, a geological marvel on which you will be required to write a brief essay on Monday morning.

That is all. Have a pleasant day, and try to behave yourselves in a manner to bring credit to the college.

The Revelation of Jesus Christ is not a book intended to be observed but experienced, over and over. It is designed to resonate. It is offensive to the cultured sensibilities which shield us because it is supposed to transcend them, to speak not only *to* us but *through* us. Many of those who have given themselves to it whole-heartedly are seldom seen again. They are devoured. They become alien. They speak a new language, the "madness" of the prophets whose eyes see the chariots of God (2 Kings 6:17).

Although it appears to be a hostile and foreign landscape filled with confronting symbols, animal totems, virginal sacrifices clad in pure white, chosen, slain and ascending with a disturbing sexual undercurrent, the Revelation is in fact the authentic end of the story, a denouement of the natural world. The seed, flesh and skin of Genesis is everywhere in the Revelation, employed to express the bestial nature and hidden nakedness of institutions masquerading as gods and goddesses. The primeval world of Adam, a barren landscape of widows and orphans, is not a Dreamtime but a *history*. Ridiculed, ignored and neglected, it waits silently until the sixth hour, when time shall be no more. The fruits of culture are ripe, and it bites and devours, consumes and transfigures. Revelation is Genesis at full throttle, a bottle to be consumed and be consumed by, a fruit once forbidden but now freely offered. It is a book which removes inhibitions and exposes the hidden intents of the heart. The gardens of men are theft and nakedness, their lands are murder, and their cities are exile. The pungent, Dreamtime symbols are the hidden reality. The grotesque totems are a tangible exposure of "what we see and what we seem."

Yet, as with the controversial Chapter 18 of *Picnic At Hanging Rock,* the Revelation contains nothing that is not contained either explicitly or implicitly in the earlier parts of the story. It simply describes the natural world condemned in Romans 1 and 2 in a different language, one which is impossible to explain or contain within the Victorian corset of Western Christianity. As John Taylor writes in his introduction to Chapter 18 in *The Secret of Hanging Rock*:

> As anyone can see, the chapter is quite unfilmable. Film can only work with what God gives it, and God did not give it the same elasticity He granted the novel—though people keep trying, as the cutting-room floor shows.

It is little wonder that the "schoolgirls" of modern Bible colleges are constrained to the safety of the lower slopes by the prim widows of worldly academia.

COVENANT-LITERARY TEMPLATES

Following are the most common and helpful instances of the "hive" structure of the Bible. It is this which underlies all my thinking concerning the Scriptures.

I believe we must identify the structure (forming) if we are to understand the glory (filling).

Creation

Division

Ascension

Testing

Maturity

Conquest

Glorification

CREATION

Creation - **Day 1:**
Light - Night and Day

FORMING

Division - **Day 2:**
Waters - Above and Below

Ascension - **Day 3:**
Dry Land, Grain and Fruit

Testing - **Day 4:**
Ruling Lights

FILLING

Maturity - **Day 5:**
Birds and Fish

Conquest - **Day 6:**
Animals and Man

FUTURE

Glorification - **Day 7:**
Rest and Rule

TABERNACLE

Creation - **Ark of the Covenant:**
The Law written on stone

    Division - **Veil:**
    The face of God veiled

        Ascension -
        Bronze Altar:
        The Adamic body formed
        and Golden Table:
        The face of Adam presented

            Testing - **Lampstand:**
            The eyes of God opened

        Maturity - **Incense Altar:**
        The Evian body formed

    Conquest - **Sacrifices & High Priest:**
    The face of God unveiled

Glorification - **Shekinah:**
The Law written on flesh

SACRIFICE

DE-FORMING

 Creation - **Called:**
Animal chosen

Division - **Sanctified:**
Animal separated / sacrifice cut

Ascension - **Presented:**
Sacrifice lifted onto Altar
Sacrifice awaits

DE-FILLING

Testing - **Purified:**
Holy fire descends

Maturity - **Transformed:**
Clouds of fragrant Smoke

Conquest - **Vindicated:**
The savor accepted by God

FUTURE

Glorification - **Sent:**
Reconciliation and reunion

FEASTS

Creation - **Sabbath:**
Weekly rest - House of Israel

Division - **Passover:**
Sin removed (external Law)

Ascension - **Firstfruits:**
Israel as Priest

Testing - **Pentecost:**
Israel as King

Maturity - **Trumpets:**
Israel as Prophet

Conquest - **Atonement:**
Sin removed (internal Law)

Glorification - **Booths (Ingathering):**
Annual rest - House of all nations

DOMINION

Creation - **Genesis:**
Israel called from the nations

Division - **Exodus:**
Israel cut from the nations

Ascension - **Leviticus:**
Israel presented to God (Man)

Testing - **Numbers:**
Israel threshed (People)

Maturity - **Deuteronomy:**
Israel reassembled (Army)

Conquest - **Joshua:**
The nations cut from the Land

Glorification - **Judges:**
Israel among the nations

CREATION	DOMINION	FEASTS
Day 1 Light - Night & Day *(Ark of the Covenant)*	**Genesis** *Creation*	**Sabbath** (promise of rest) *God's rest*
Day 2 Waters divided *(Veil)*	**Exodus** *Division*	**Passover** (sin covered) *Adam's sin removed*
Day 3 Dry Land, Grain & Fruit *(Altar & Table)*	**Leviticus** *Ascension*	**Firstfruits** (priesthood) *Adam brought to God*
Day 4 Ruling Lights *(Lampstand)*	**Numbers** *Testing*	**Pentecost** (harvest) *Law revealed*
Day 5 Birds & Fish *(Incense Altar)*	**Deuteronomy** *Maturity*	**Trumpets** (armies) *Eve brought to God*
Day 6 Animals & Man *(Mediators: High)* *Priest & Sacrifices)*	**Joshua** *Conquest*	**Atonement** (sin expelled) *Eve removed from sin*
Day 7 Rest & Ruling *(Shekinah Glory)*	**Judges** *Glorification*	**Booths** (ingathering) *Adam's rest*

COVENANT

<u>TRANSCENDENCE</u> - "Who's the boss?"

 Creation - **Initiation:**
God begins a new era in history

<u>HIERARCHY</u> - "Whom has he put in charge?"

 Division - **Delegation:**
He sets apart His representatives

<u>ETHICS (LAW)</u> - "What are the rules?"

 Ascension - **Presentation:**
Law is given to them

 Testing - **Purification:**
Law is opened to them

 Maturity - **Transformation:**
Law is received by them

<u>OATH/SANCTIONS</u> - "What are the rewards?"

 Conquest - **Vindication:**
His representatives submit to
God's blessing or cursing

<u>SUCCESSION</u> - "What's next?"

 Glorification - **Representation:**
The faithful are commissioned as rulers
and given an inheritance in history

FORMING

FILLING

FUTURE

TEN WORDS

FORMING	FILLING
(Head - Adam - Priest)	*(Body - Eve - People)*

TRANSCENDENCE

ABOVE	**1** Word from God *False Gods*	**2** Word to God *False Oath*

HIERARCHY

3 Work *Sabbath*	**4** Land *Father and Mother*

BESIDE	*KNIFE*	ETHICS	*FIRE*
	5 Murder *Sons of God*		**6** Adultery *Daughters of Men*

SANCTIONS

7 Stealing *False Blessings*	**8** False Witness *False Curses*

SUCCESSION

BELOW	**9** Coveting Shelter *Formed House*	**10** Coveting the Sheltered *Filled House*

1 See *Bible Matrix II: The Covenant Key*, Chapter 4, for an explanation of why I have arranged the Ten Words in this fashion.

FOOD LAWS

ADAM'S PROHIBITION

Creation - **Initiation:**
Springs water the Land,
but there is no Man.

   Division - **Delegation:**
   Adam is formed out of the dust,

      Ascension - **Presentation:**
      given a single, temporary
      PROHIBITION, then broken
      and opened to construct Eve.

         Testing - **Purification:**
         The serpent seduces Eve.
         Adam and Eve eat, and their
         eyes are opened.

      Maturity - **Transformation:**
      The PROHIBITION is now
      obsolete. They attempt to hide
      their nakedness.

   Conquest - **Vindication:**
   and are judged by the Lord. Innocent
   substitutes are de-formed.

Glorification - **Representation:**
Instead of ingathering, there is scattering.

EVE'S PROHIBITIONS

Creation - **Initiation:**
Rivers of blood (genealogy and sacrifice) flow
from Eden but there is no mediatorial Man.

Division - **Delegation:**
Israel is formed out of a barren
womb *(Circumcision)*,

Ascension - **Presentation:**
raised up and put into the Land.
They are given many temporary
PROHIBITIONS, then broken in
two, opened to build a new Body.

Testing - **Purification:**
Christ defeats the serpent
and opens the Church's eyes.

Maturity - **Transformation:**
The PROHIBITIONS become
obsolete. The Firstfruits Church is
robed in white, witnesses boldly,

Conquest - **Vindication:**
and Herodian worship is judged by the
Lord. Old Covenant Israel is de-formed.
(un-Circumcision)

Glorification - **Representation:**
Under the Married Mediatorial Man, rivers of
living water flow out into all the nations.

ISRAEL

DAY 1 - LIGHT
Creation - **Patriarchs, Abraham:**
Light dawns upon the "waters" of the 70 nations

DAY 2 - WATERS DIVIDED
Division - **Exodus Moses:**
Israel is separated to mediate for the nations

DAY 3 - DRY LAND
Ascension - **Promised Land, Joshua:**
Israel possesses the Land

DAY 4 - RULING LIGHTS
Testing - **David & Solomon:**
Mighty men rule under God

DAY 5 - SWARMS
Maturity - **Captivity to Gentiles:**
The prophets witness to the kings.
Gentile armies plague Land and Sea

DAY 6 - MEDIATORS
Conquest - **Joshua the High Priest, to Jesus:**
Israel ministers within the *oikoumene*.

DAY 7 - REST & RULE
Glorification - **Jesus and the Church:**
The saints receive the kingdom and judge the Land.

THE LAST DAYS

TRANSCENDENCE

Creation - **Perfect Life of Christ**
Peace on earth *(Sabbath)*

HIERARCHY

Division - **Perfect Death of Christ**
Nakedness, flesh torn *(Passover)*

ETHICS (LAW)

Ascension - **Rule of Christ (AD30)**
Jesus rules at the Father's right hand
(Firstfruits)

Testing - **Sending of the Spirit**
The harvest begins *(Pentecost)*

Maturity - **Witness of the Apostles**
A Jew-Gentile Body mustered
(Trumpets)

OATH/SANCTIONS

Conquest - **Temple Destroyed (AD70)**
All righteous blood avenged *(Atonement)*

SUCCESSION

Glorification - **Priestly Rule of the Church**
Gospel carried to all nations *(Booths)*

GARDEN

LAND

WORLD

HISTORY

TRANSCENDENCE

Creation - **Adam to Noah:**
World united as one blood

HIERARCHY

Division - **Abraham to Joseph:**
World divided by blood *(Circumcision)*

ETHICS (LAW)

Ascension - **Moses to AD30:**[2]
Centralized priesthood
EARTHLY MEDIATORS

Testing - **Christ:**
The harvest begins

Maturity - **Christ to AD70:**[3]
Centralized priesthood
HEAVENLY MEDIATORS

OATH/SANCTIONS

Conquest - **AD70 to final judgment:**
World divided by water *(Baptism)*

SUCCESSION

Glorification - **final judgment:**
World united by one Spirit

---

2   The death of Christ.
3   The destruction of the Jewish Temple and the city of Jerusalem.

Made in the USA
San Bernardino, CA
02 June 2015